NAVIGATING QUALITY ENGINEERING IN THE AI ERA

Key Insights for Modern Quality
Engineering and Management

EVGENY TKACHENKO

NAVIGATING QUALITY ENGINEERING

IN THE AI ERA

Copyright © 2024 by Evgeny Tkachenko

All rights reserved.

No part of this book may be reproduced or used in any manner without the written permission of the copyright owner except for the use of quotations in a book review.

ISBN 9798329381856

Printed in the United States of America

Edition 1.05

CONTENTS

INTRODUCTION..1
CHAPTER 1. FOUNDATIONS OF QUALITY ENGINEERING
    Introduction to Quality Engineering....................6
    Evolution of Quality Management....................... 8
    The Shift Left Paradigm.......................................10
    Personal Story: Applying Scrum And Shift Left Outside Of Work.. 16

CHAPTER 2. TECHNIQUES AND STRATEGIES IN QUALITY ENGINEERING
    Agile in Quality Engineering............................. 22
    Quality Assurance Techniques........................... 25
    Devops in Quality Engineering..........................43
    Continuous Testing..46
    Personal Story: Transitioning From the Ice-cream Cone to a Balanced Testing Approach..................49

CHAPTER 3. CHALLENGES AND SOLUTIONS IN QUALITY ENGINEERING
    Embracing the Shift Left Paradigm....................56
    Quality Metrics as Your Compass......................74
    Leveraging Automation and AI in Quality Engineering..83
    Hiring and Developing Quality Engineers.......... 86
    Personal Story: the Transformation Challenge...94

CHAPTER 4. FUTURE TRENDS AND INNOVATIONS
    The Impact of AI on Quality Engineering......... 102
    The Role of Quality Engineers as Enablers....... 106

Transforming Quality Managers..........................112
Ethical Considerations in AI and Quality
Engineering..115
Personal Story: How AI Revolutionized My Role
as Head of Quality Engineering........................... 119
CONCLUSION... 123
ABOUT THE AUTHOR..127
ACKNOWLEDGEMENTS...................................... 129
SOURCES..131

INTRODUCTION

In today's rapidly evolving technological landscape, the roles and responsibilities of quality engineering and management are undergoing significant transformation. The shift towards agile and DevOps methodologies, the advent of artificial intelligence (AI), and the increasing demand for faster, higher-quality software delivery have all contributed to redefining how quality is perceived and achieved in software development.

This book, "Navigating Quality Engineering in the AI Era," explores critical aspects of quality engineering and management, drawing on insights and expertise from my experience with various companies. It offers practical guidance, strategic frameworks, and real-world examples to help professionals navigate this complex field.

FOUNDATIONS OF QUALITY ENGINEERING

The journey begins by examining the historical foundations of quality engineering and tracing its evolution through traditional quality assurance practices to modern principles such as "Shift Left" testing and continuous testing. We explore how these shifts have transformed quality engineering into a proactive, collaborative, and integral part of the development process.

TECHNIQUES AND STRATEGIES IN QUALITY ENGINEERING

In the new paradigm of Shift Left, QEs play a pivotal role in promoting quality from the outset of the development cycle. We outline their mission as architects of quality, collaborators, and advocates for leading practices. Emphasizing the importance of early testing, automation, and continuous learning, we explore how QEs empower teams to deliver high-quality software efficiently.

CHALLENGES AND SOLUTIONS IN QUALITY ENGINEERING

Change is constant in the world of software development, and Quality Engineers (QEs) are at the forefront of experiencing and navigating these transformations, playing a key role in fostering collaboration and driving successful organizational change. Through real-life examples, we delve into the common challenges faced by QEs and explore strategies to overcome resistance, foster collaboration, and achieve quality excellence. We also explore the evolving role of QEs as enablers with DevOps knowledge and the transformation of Quality Managers into technical leaders driving excellence and fostering a culture of quality.

FUTURE TRENDS AND INNOVATIONS

Artificial intelligence is revolutionizing quality engineering, introducing new tools and techniques that enhance efficiency and effectiveness. We discuss how AI is transforming QE jobs, from automated testing and intelligent defect management to predictive analytics and continuous testing. Emphasizing the need for skill enhancement and adaptation, we highlight how QE professionals can embrace AI technologies to drive continuous improvement in software quality assurance.

"Navigating Quality Engineering in the AI Era" serves as a guide for quality engineering professionals, offering insights, strategies, and practical advice to thrive amidst constant technological change. By embracing the principles outlined in this book, QEs and Quality Managers can confidently navigate the complexities of modern software development and drive excellence in software quality assurance.

Welcome to the journey of navigating quality engineering in the AI era. Let's embark on this transformative path together.

CHAPTER 1

FOUNDATIONS OF QUALITY ENGINEERING

INTRODUCTION TO QUALITY ENGINEERING

Quality Engineering (QE) represents a multifaceted discipline vital to maintaining the integrity and reliability of software products across industries. Embracing a comprehensive blend of quality assurance (QA) practices and testing methodologies, QE serves as a cornerstone in modern software development processes. In today's swiftly evolving digital landscape, the significance of QE has surged dramatically, necessitating a paradigm shift from conventional testing approaches to a proactive, integrated methodology.

At its essence, QE transcends the traditional role of testing performed merely at the conclusion of the development lifecycle. Instead, it fosters a proactive stance throughout every phase of software development. QE professionals collaborate intimately with developers, product managers, and stakeholders right from project inception. This early involvement facilitates the embedding of rigorous quality standards and practices from the project's outset, thereby mitigating risks and enhancing overall product reliability.

Fundamentally, QE is underpinned by a commitment to proactive quality management and continual enhancement. This involves strategically combining manual and automated testing methodologies, rigorous risk assessment frameworks, process refinement initiatives, and unwavering adherence to industry standards and leading practices. By integrating these elements, QE endeavors to preemptively identify and rectify potential defects, streamline development workflows, and uphold stringent quality benchmarks.

In tandem with the widespread adoption of agile methodologies and DevOps practices, the role of Quality Engineers has undergone a profound evolution. Beyond conventional testing responsibilities, QE professionals now assume pivotal roles in spearheading initiatives such as test automation, continuous integration and delivery/deployment (CI/CD), and fostering cross-functional collaboration. This transformative shift underscores the imperative of seamlessly integrating quality assurance across the entire software development lifecycle, thus ensuring the swift delivery of software products that meet the exacting demands of contemporary users.

As organizations navigate the dynamic terrain of digital transformation, QE emerges not merely as a requisite function but as a transformative force driving operational excellence and customer satisfaction. By embracing QE principles, organizations fortify their capacity to innovate swiftly, deliver robust software solutions, and sustain competitive advantage in an increasingly interconnected global marketplace.

EVOLUTION OF QUALITY MANAGEMENT

The landscape of Quality Management has undergone a profound evolution over recent decades, driven by technological advancements, shifting paradigms in software development, and the imperative for enhanced efficiency and reliability in delivering software products.

Historically, Quality Management predominantly revolved around post-development testing and quality assurance (QA) activities. In the traditional Waterfall model, software development proceeded sequentially through phases, with testing relegated to a distinct phase following development completion. This approach, characterized by its linear progression, often resulted in the identification of defects late in the cycle, necessitating extensive rework and causing project delays and cost overruns.

The shortcomings of the Waterfall model became increasingly evident as software complexity grew and market demands for faster delivery and higher quality intensified. This led to the rise of agile methodologies, heralding a paradigm shift in Quality Management. Agile frameworks like Scrum and Kanban focus on iterative development, continuous feedback loops, and fostering close collaboration among developers, testers, and stakeholders throughout the entire development lifecycle. Some teams I have worked with were even more effective following a mixed framework called Scrumban.

In the agile context, testing ceases to be a standalone phase and is integrated seamlessly into every iteration or sprint. This integration enables early detection and resolution of defects, fostering a culture of continuous improvement and embedding quality into the software from its inception.

The emergence of DevOps further accelerated the evolution of Quality Management practices. DevOps represents a cultural and operational shift that aims to unify development (Dev) and operations (Ops) teams through automation, collaboration, and shared responsibility. Central to DevOps is the concept of continuous integration and continuous delivery/deployment (CI/CD), where changes to code are automatically built, tested, and prepared for deployment in a rapid and reliable manner. In Continuous Delivery (CD), the software build is delivered automatically after testing, allowing a human decision on deployment. In Continuous Deployment (CD), changes are automatically deployed to customers or users without manual intervention.

DevOps practices not only facilitate faster delivery cycles but also promote a holistic approach to quality throughout the software delivery pipeline. By automating testing, configuration management, and infrastructure provisioning, DevOps minimizes human error, accelerates feedback loops, and enhances overall product stability and reliability.

This evolution signifies a transition from reactive to proactive Quality Management. Quality Engineers, once relegated to the role of testers at the end of the development cycle, are now integral members of cross-functional agile teams. They advocate for leading practices, facilitate collaboration between developers and operations, and champion continuous improvement initiatives aimed at optimizing processes and enhancing product quality.

In essence, the evolution of Quality Management reflects a broader industry shift towards embracing agility, DevOps practices, and a proactive approach to quality assurance. By incorporating testing and quality processes earlier in the development lifecycle and promoting collaboration and continuous improvement, organizations are better equipped to deliver software products that meet the rigorous demands of today's dynamic market.

THE SHIFT LEFT PARADIGM

"We cannot rely on mass inspection to improve quality, though there are times when 100 percent inspection is necessary. As Harold S. Dodge said many years ago, 'You cannot inspect quality into a product.' The quality is there or it isn't by the time it's inspected."

--Dr. W. Edwards Deming. *Out of the Crisis*

Inspection to enhance quality is often delayed, inefficient, and expensive. Dr. Deming stated, "Inspection, scrap, downgrading, and rework are not corrective actions on the process. Rework raises costs." He implies that enhancing processes to prevent defects and rework is a more effective way to lower costs. Similarly, Philip B. Crosby in his book "Quality is Free" echoes this sentiment, stating, "Quality is free. It's not a gift, but it's free. The 'unquality' things are what cost money."

One issue that persistently troubled Dr. Deming was management's belief that higher quality justified higher pricing. Dr. Deming, however, argued that quality not only reduces costs but should also lead to lower pricing.

Quality is not additive; it cannot be added at the end of the line. Quality must be built into every stage of the production process. Quality comes not from inspection but from improving the production process itself. That is why we need to invest in tools and processes that help us prevent defects as early as possible. I'm sure you've all heard the phrase 'everyone should own quality' regarding your projects, and this sentiment is increasingly prevalent these days. The concept of 'Shift Left' has emerged as a pivotal strategy in modern software development, reshaping how organizations approach quality assurance (QA) and testing. This paradigm promotes conducting quality assurance activities at the beginning of the software development lifecycle, with the goal of identifying and addressing issues at their inception rather than in the later stages of development.

In summary, traditionally, testing and QA were relegated to the end of the development cycle in a sequential manner, often resulting in the accumulation of defects that required significant resources and time to address. The Shift Left approach challenges this norm by integrating testing activities right from the beginning, aligning them closely with each phase of development.

Key Principles of Shift Left

1. **Early Testing and Test Design.** Shift Left promotes the initiation of both test design and testing activities at the outset of the development process. This includes planning and designing unit tests, integration tests, and other forms of testing to detect and rectify defects as soon as they arise. By catching issues early through thorough test design and execution, teams can prevent them from escalating into more complex problems later on.

2. **Collaboration.** A cornerstone of Shift Left is fostering collaboration between different teams involved in software development, including developers, testers, and operations. By establishing clear communication channels and a shared understanding of quality expectations from the project's inception, teams can work together effectively to deliver high-quality software. Methodologies like Behavior-Driven Development (BDD) further enhance this collaboration by using plain language to define the behavior of the software. This helps ensure that all stakeholders, including non-technical team members, are on the same page and understand the requirements and expectations, leading to fewer misunderstandings and more cohesive teamwork.
3. **Automation.** Automation plays a crucial role in enabling Shift Left practices. Integrated into the development pipeline, automated testing tools and frameworks streamline repetitive testing tasks and support continuous testing. This automation not only accelerates the testing process but also enhances reliability and consistency in executing tests, thereby helping to identify defects more efficiently.
4. **Continuous Integration and Continuous Delivery/Deployment (CI/CD).** Embracing CI/CD practices is integral to Shift

Left. These practices automate the building, testing, and deployment of code changes, facilitating continuous integration, testing, and delivery of software updates to production environments. This rapid feedback loop enables teams to address issues promptly and deliver updates efficiently.

5. **Risk Identification and Mitigation.** Shift Left emphasizes proactive risk management. Teams prioritize early identification and mitigation of risks, potential issues, and defects throughout the development lifecycle. This includes thorough requirements analysis and testing to confirm that all aspects of the project's requirements are understood, feasible, and testable. By conducting risk assessments early on, teams can implement preemptive measures to mitigate risks and enhance product reliability. Early and continuous requirements testing helps catch potential issues before they evolve into significant problems, contributing to a more stable and reliable software product.

6. **Prevention over Detection.** Unlike traditional approaches focused on defect detection, Shift Left emphasizes prevention. Teams adopt proactive measures and implement quality practices and standards from the outset to minimize the occurrence of defects. This mindset shift leads to improved software quality and reduces the need for

costly rework. Additionally, conducting post-mortem meetings and root cause analysis after incidents helps teams identify the underlying causes of defects and implement strategies to prevent similar issues in the future. By learning from past mistakes and continuously improving processes, teams can significantly enhance their defect prevention capabilities.
7. **Empowering Developers.** In the Shift Left paradigm, developers are empowered to take ownership of testing and quality assurance aspects. They actively participate in writing unit tests and, in some cases, integration and system-level tests. This helps to maintain code quality and fosters collaboration with QE teams.

Cultural Shift and Benefits

Shift Left represents more than just a methodology; it embodies a cultural shift towards a more collaborative and efficient approach to software development. By incorporating collaboration, quality assurance, and testing from the early stages of development, organizations can improve overall product quality, expedite time-to-market, and foster a development environment that is more responsive to evolving user demands.

In conclusion, the Shift Left paradigm aligns with the foundational principles of Quality Engineering, emphasizing proactive quality management, continuous improvement, and collaborative software development practices. As organizations navigate the complexities of modern software delivery, embracing Shift Left principles will be crucial in delivering high-quality software products that meet and exceed user expectations.

PERSONAL STORY: APPLYING SCRUM AND SHIFT LEFT OUTSIDE OF WORK

Embarking on a major life change, such as relocating to another country, can be as complex and demanding as any large-scale project in the workplace. When my wife and I faced the daunting task of moving to the U.S., I found myself drawing on my professional experience in Quality Engineering. Intrigued by the potential of Agile methodologies to streamline and optimize processes, I decided to experiment with applying these principles—specifically Scrum and the Shift Left approach—to organize and manage our move effectively. Here's an overview of how we integrated these transformative strategies into our personal life planning:

Setting Up the Kanban Board

To start, we created a virtual Kanban board to visually manage our tasks. This board had columns for tasks to do, tasks in progress, and tasks done. We listed all the tasks we could think of, from securing visas and booking flights to arranging for our belongings to be shipped and finding accommodation in the US. Each task was treated as a "story" with clear requirements and deadlines.

Planning and Preparatory Research

Early in our moving process, we recognized the importance of meticulous planning and preemptive research. By identifying potential issues and understanding our needs, we were able to set realistic deadlines and incorporate buffer times for any unforeseen delays. For instance, we conducted an early survey of the housing market in the state we were moving to, which allowed us to determine where we wanted to live and to confirm we had the necessary budget in place.

Daily Check-In Meetings

Unlike typical morning stand-up meetings in Scrum, we held our check-ins in the evening, after work. During these meetings, we reviewed our Kanban board, moving tasks from 'to do' to 'in progress' and eventually to 'done.' This routine helped us stay organized and keep track of our progress. We also prioritized tasks based on urgency and impact, addressing critical items first. Evening meetings worked better for us because they allowed us to reflect on the day's activities and plan more effectively for the next day.

Handling Dependencies and Emergencies

As with any complex project, we encountered tasks that were dependent on external factors. For example, when we discovered we had missed a vaccination requirement for our cat, we had to prioritize this task urgently. We paused other activities and focused on finding a vet clinic that could provide the necessary vaccination quickly. This incident underscored the importance of early requirements analysis and being prepared for unforeseen issues.

Lessons Learned

This experience of using Scrum and Shift Left principles in our personal project taught us valuable lessons:

- Proactive Planning. The importance of thorough requirements analysis early in the process cannot be overstated. This approach helped us anticipate potential issues and address them before they became critical.
- Flexibility and Prioritization. Having a flexible approach allowed us to switch tasks and prioritize urgent issues without losing sight of our overall progress.
- Daily Coordination. Regular check-ins kept us aligned and informed, ensuring we were always aware of our progress and any emerging issues.

Successful Outcome

By the time we completed our relocation, we had successfully managed all aspects of the move without major issues. This experience not only strengthened our belief in the effectiveness of Agile methodologies but also highlighted the benefits of the Shift Left approach in both professional and personal projects.

Since then, I have enjoyed applying these methodologies in various aspects of my life, reaffirming their value in managing complex and uncertain projects efficiently.

CHAPTER 2

TECHNIQUES AND STRATEGIES IN QUALITY ENGINEERING

The landscape of software development has been profoundly transformed by Agile and DevOps methodologies. Both paradigms emphasize speed, flexibility, and collaboration, making them highly compatible with modern Quality Engineering (QE) practices.

AGILE IN QUALITY ENGINEERING

Agile methodologies have revolutionized software development by emphasizing flexibility, collaboration, and continuous improvement. Quality Engineering (QE) practices have seamlessly integrated with Agile principles to enhance software quality, accelerate delivery, and foster a culture of collaboration across development teams.

Iterative Testing

One of the core principles of Agile in QE is iterative testing. In Agile frameworks such as Scrum or Scrumban, development work is organized into short, time-boxed iterations or sprints. During each sprint, testing activities run concurrently with development tasks. This iterative approach allows QE teams to detect defects early in the development process, facilitating their timely resolution before they can escalate into more critical issues. By conducting frequent testing iterations, Agile methodologies facilitate the continuous monitoring and improvement of software quality throughout the project lifecycle.

Collaboration

Agile methodologies promote a collaborative environment where cross-functional teams, including developers, testers, product owners, and stakeholders, work closely together throughout the development cycle. This collaboration is essential for aligning on quality goals, understanding project requirements, and helping to ensure that the software meets user expectations. QE professionals actively engage in Agile ceremonies such as daily stand-ups, sprint planning meetings, and retrospectives to share insights, address challenges, and refine testing strategies based on real-time feedback from development teams.

Flexibility

Agile's adaptive nature is another cornerstone of its integration with QE. Unlike traditional Waterfall approaches, Agile methodologies support adaptability and embrace evolving requirements throughout the entire project lifecycle. QE teams leverage this flexibility to adjust testing strategies, prioritize test cases, and respond promptly to emerging issues or shifts in project priorities. By continuously adapting their testing efforts to align with changing project dynamics, Agile QE teams optimize resource allocation and align testing efforts with overall project goals.

Incremental Quality Improvement

Agile methodologies promote incremental delivery of software functionality, accompanied by continuous feedback loops and iterative improvements. This incremental approach extends to quality assurance practices, where QE teams focus on incrementally enhancing software quality throughout each sprint. Continuous feedback from stakeholders and end-users guides QE professionals in refining test cases, validating functionality, and identifying areas for further optimization. By prioritizing incremental quality improvements, Agile QE teams mitigate the risk of major defects emerging in later stages of development, thereby enhancing overall product reliability and user satisfaction.

Incorporating Agile methodologies into Quality Engineering practices has proven instrumental in fostering collaboration, accelerating delivery, and maintaining high standards of software quality. By embracing iterative testing, promoting collaboration across teams, leveraging flexibility to adapt to changing requirements, and prioritizing incremental quality improvement, Agile QE teams are well-positioned to meet the evolving demands of today's dynamic software development landscape.

QUALITY ASSURANCE TECHNIQUES

Quality Assurance (QA) techniques play a pivotal role in ensuring that software products meet specified quality standards, adhere to requirements, and deliver exceptional user experiences. These techniques encompass both manual (hands-on) and automated approaches, each serving distinct purposes in the software development lifecycle.

Manual (Hands-on) Testing

Manual testing, often referred to as hands-on testing, involves testers actively interacting with the software application to identify defects without the use of automated tools. This approach relies on the tester's expertise, intuition, and creativity to explore the software's functionality, usability, and performance from an end-user perspective. It allows for a more nuanced and flexible evaluation of the software, as human testers can adapt to unexpected behaviors and provide valuable insights that automated tests might miss.

In this context, I use the term "Manual Testing" to mean hands-on testing. Notably, Michael Bolton has critiqued the term "manual testing," arguing that it undermines the value of the craft. He emphasizes that testing is a thoughtful and skilled activity, not merely a manual task.

By using the term "Manual Testing" in this book, I refer to the intricate, hands-on process that leverages human insight and expertise to ensure software quality.

When Manual Testing is Often Done

1. **Exploratory Testing**
   - Description: Testers dynamically and intuitively explore the software application without predefined scripts. This approach is particularly effective in uncovering unexpected defects and evaluating the software's behavior under varying conditions.
   - Purpose: To identify issues that are not covered by formal test cases, understanding the application from a user's perspective.
   - Process: Testers are given the freedom to interact with the application in a non-linear fashion, guided by their knowledge, experience, and curiosity.
   - Tour Testing: A type of exploratory testing introduced by James Whittaker. Tour testing involves testers taking a "tour" of the application with specific goals or themes in mind, such as checking for common user errors or security vulnerabilities. This approach helps uncover issues that might not be

evident through more structured testing methods.

2. **Ad-hoc Testing**
   - Description: Informal testing where testers execute spontaneous tests based on their intuition and experience, often revealing critical defects that might not be captured through scripted tests.
   - Purpose: To quickly identify significant issues without the constraints of predefined test cases.
   - Process: Testers use their knowledge of the application and its potential problem areas to conduct impromptu tests, focusing on areas they suspect might be problematic. While both ad-hoc and exploratory testing involve a degree of spontaneity, exploratory testing is a more disciplined and systematic approach that combines test design, execution, and learning. Ad-hoc testing, on the other hand, is more random and informal, often relying on the tester's intuition and experience.

3. **Usability Testing**
   - Description: Usability testing evaluates the user interface (UI) and user experience (UX) aspects of the software to ensure it is intuitive, easy to navigate, and meets user expectations.

- Purpose: The primary goal is to prioritize user-friendliness and deliver a satisfactory user experience with the software.
- Process: Involves having real users perform tasks with the software while Quality Engineers (QEs) observe. This helps identify usability issues, gather user feedback, and make necessary improvements. Key aspects evaluated include design, layout, navigation, and overall interaction experience.
- Observation by QEs: Usability testing is usually performed by real users with QEs observing to gain insights into user interactions, understand pain points, and gather feedback for improvements.

4. **Regression Testing**
   - **Description:** Regression testing involves re-running tests that were previously run on the existing system.
   - Purpose: The primary purpose of regression testing is to verify that new code changes have not adversely affected the existing functionality of the software or inadvertently introduced defects.
   - Process: Testers re-execute a subset of tests that had previously passed, possibly concentrating on the areas of the application that have been modified

or are at risk of being affected by recent changes.
- o Automation Considerations: While regression testing is typically automated to improve efficiency and consistency, some cases may remain manual due to various reasons. Certain scenarios might not be feasible for automation due to their complexity, dynamic nature, or because automating them would not provide a significant return on investment (ROI). In such cases, manual regression testing can help provide validation of critical functionalities and areas of the application.

Automated Testing

Automation has revolutionized Quality Engineering (QE), enabling rapid and consistent execution of tests across software applications. Automated testing involves the use of specialized software tools to execute predefined test cases and compare actual outcomes with expected results automatically. This approach plays a crucial role in QE by achieving high test coverage and ensuring that tests are executed consistently and reliably throughout the software development lifecycle.

Key Benefits of Automated Testing

1. **Speed.** Automated testing allows for significantly quicker execution compared to manual testing, which enables Quality Engineering (QE) teams to conduct more frequent testing and receive prompt feedback on the software's quality.
2. **Consistency and Reliability.** Automated tests deliver reliable and repeatable outcomes, which significantly reduces the likelihood of human error. They also ensure that testing is carried out in a controlled and consistent environment.
3. **Scalability.** Automation allows for extensive test coverage by enabling the execution of a large number of tests across different environments, devices, and configurations simultaneously. This capability is particularly valuable for regression testing, where verifying that new code changes do not harm existing functionality is essential. Beyond regression testing, automated testing can also encompass performance, load, and integration testing, and more, thereby providing a comprehensive evaluation of the software's stability and performance. With automation, tests can be run more frequently and efficiently, allowing for continuous testing and integration within the development pipeline. This scalability allows the testing process to keep pace as the

software grows and evolves, maintaining high-quality standards without a proportional increase in manual testing effort.
4. **Efficiency.** By automating repetitive testing tasks, QE resources are freed up to focus on exploratory testing activities, or other types of testing such as usability testing or performance testing, thereby improving overall testing efficiency.

Risks, Disadvantages, and Costs of Automated Testing

Initial Investment. Setting up automated testing requires a significant upfront investment in terms of tools, infrastructure, and training. This may include the cost of purchasing automation tools, although many are shifting to open-source options to reduce initial costs. While open-source tools can lower upfront expenses, they often require customization and additional internal development to effectively meet specific project needs. Regardless of the tools chosen, they must be integrated into the development pipeline, and the team must be trained to use these tools effectively.

Maintenance. Automated tests require ongoing maintenance to keep up with changes in the application. As the software evolves, automated test scripts must be updated to reflect new functionality and changes in the user interface, which can be time-consuming and resource-intensive, particularly if investment in the structure of the automated tests was inadequate.

Tool Dependency. Heavy reliance on automated testing tools can limit flexibility. Changes in tool licensing, support, or capabilities can impact the overall testing strategy and may require significant adjustments if switching to a different tool becomes necessary.

Complexity. Not all tests are suitable for automation. Complex test scenarios, particularly those involving extensive user interaction or those that are highly dynamic, may be difficult to automate effectively. This can lead to incomplete test coverage or the need to maintain a hybrid approach combining both automated and manual testing.

By acknowledging both the benefits and the potential downsides of automated testing, organizations can make informed decisions about how to best integrate automation into their QE processes, balancing efficiency and effectiveness with practical considerations and constraints.

Key Types of Automated Testing

1. **Unit Testing.** Automated tests validate individual units or components of the software in isolation, confirming they function correctly as per design specifications. These tests are the

foundation of any test automation strategy and are typically the most granular, focusing on the smallest pieces of code, such as functions or methods.
2. **Integration Testing.** Automated tests verify the interaction and integration between different modules or components within the software system, validating data communication and functionality flow. Integration tests ensure that combined parts of an application work together as expected.
3. **System Testing.** Automated tests evaluate the entire software system's functionality against specified requirements and user scenarios, confirming that all integrated components work seamlessly together. These tests cover end-to-end scenarios and validate the system as a whole.
4. **Performance Testing.** Automated tests assess the software's stability, scalability, and responsiveness under varying load scenarios, ensuring it meets performance benchmarks and user expectations. This includes load testing, stress testing, and endurance testing. This type of non-functional testing has become increasingly important after several big companies lost millions of dollars due to their services' inability to handle peak loads.
5. **Security Testing.** Automated tests identify vulnerabilities, weaknesses, and potential threats within the software application,

allowing more robust security measures to be implemented to protect sensitive data and prevent breaches. Security tests often involve simulating attacks to test the system's defenses. These tests are crucial, given the severe impact data breaches can have on a company's reputation and finances.

Typically, Quality Engineers who write functional testing scripts are not responsible for security testing, as it requires specialized skills and constant updates on current trends and vulnerabilities. In my experience, small organizations usually hire third-party companies for penetration and security testing services. In contrast, large companies typically have a dedicated department to handle cybersecurity and security testing.

To effectively manage these diverse testing types and achieve a balanced approach to quality assurance, several conceptual models (including the Agile Testing Pyramid, Testing Trophy, and Honeycomb Model) have been developed. These models guide the implementation of test automation strategies and support comprehensive software quality.

Agile Testing Pyramid

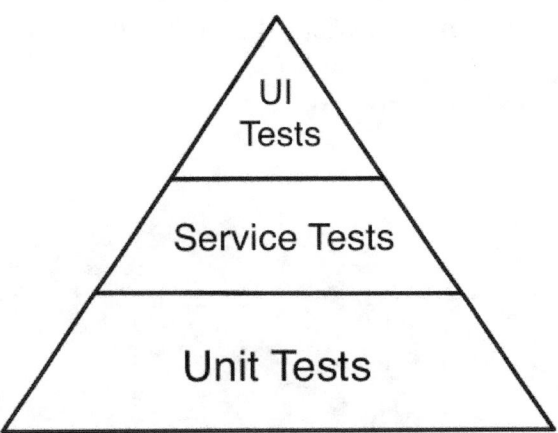

The Agile Testing Pyramid is a conceptual model that emphasizes a balanced approach to test automation by categorizing tests into three main levels. Originally introduced by Mike Cohn, this model has been popularized and expanded upon by agile testing experts Lisa Crispin and Janet Gregory.

The three levels of the pyramid are:

- **Unit Tests (Base).** The largest and most fundamental layer, consisting of numerous, fast-running tests that validate individual units (typically small, isolated pieces of code).
- **Service Tests (Middle).** Includes integration and API tests that check the interactions between components and services.

- **UI Tests (Top).** The smallest layer, containing end-to-end tests that validate the entire system through the user interface.

Testing Trophy

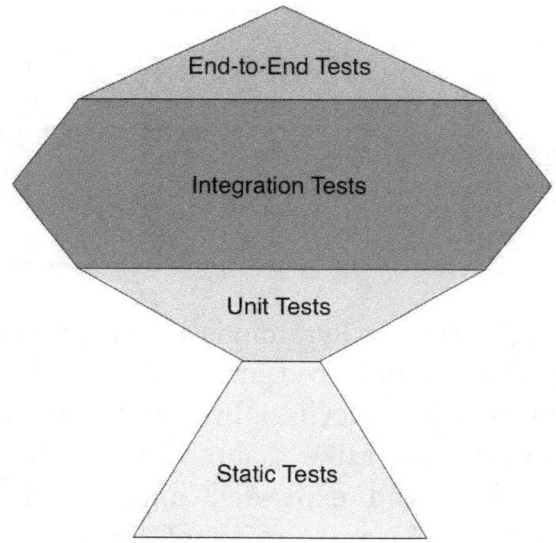

The Testing Trophy is a conceptual model introduced by Kent C. Dodds as an alternative to the Agile Testing Pyramid. It emphasizes a balanced approach to testing, highlighting the importance of different types of tests to maintain robust software quality.

The levels of the Testing Trophy are:

- **Static Tests.** This base layer involves examining the code for errors and potential issues without executing it.

- **Unit Tests.** The next layer, similar to the base of the Agile Testing Pyramid, focuses on small, isolated tests for individual functions or methods.
- **Integration Tests.** Positioned above unit tests, integration tests examine how different parts of the system interact with each other.
- **End-to-End Tests.** This top layer involves comprehensive tests that simulate real user scenarios, validating the entire system from start to finish.

Unlike the pyramid, the Testing Trophy emphasizes the importance of integration tests as a robust middle layer, ensuring that systems function correctly under various conditions and interactions.

Honeycomb Model

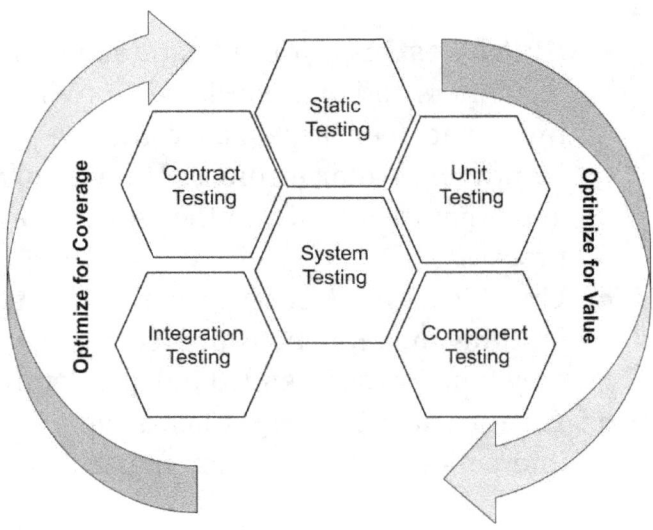

The Honeycomb Model for testing adopts Peter Morville's well-known framework that illustrates the key aspects of user experience. According to this model, each aspect is crucial for creating a comprehensive user experience, without any single aspect being inherently more important or prioritized over others by default. This approach promotes a balanced and comprehensive view of testing, emphasizing that all facets contribute equally to the quality of the user experience. It allows for flexibility, recognizing that the specific types and extent of testing required may vary depending on application specifics and business priorities.

Moreover, the model offers an expanded perspective on testing activities, acknowledging the necessity for various types of testing beyond traditional categories. Each cell in the honeycomb represents a specific testing type:

- **Static Testing.** Utilizes static analysis tools like linters and type checkers to provide immediate feedback on code quality, identifying syntax errors, code style violations, and other issues early in the development process.
- **Unit Testing.** Focuses on small, isolated tests for individual functions or methods to verify they function as intended independently.
- **Integration Testing.** Checks the interactions between different parts of the

system, verifying that integrated components work together correctly.
- **Contract Testing.** Verifies the interactions between different services or components, confirming they adhere to defined contracts or agreements. This testing ensures that changes in one service do not break functionality in another.
- **Component Testing.** Involves testing individual parts or components of a system in isolation, verifying that each component functions correctly on its own before being integrated into the larger system. Unlike unit testing, which focuses on the smallest testable parts of the code (such as functions or methods), component testing deals with larger, cohesive parts of the application, such as modules or classes, ensuring their correctness and reliability before they interact with other components.
- **System Testing.** Evaluates the entire integrated software system to ensure it meets the specified requirements. This type of testing validates the overall functionality and performance of the system in an environment that simulates production.

This representation underscores the diversity and interconnectedness of testing efforts necessary to achieve comprehensive software quality, enhancing the overall user experience by ensuring that each aspect of the system is rigorously tested and validated.

Additionally, there is a Microservices Testing Honeycomb model for microservices testing introduced by Spotify.

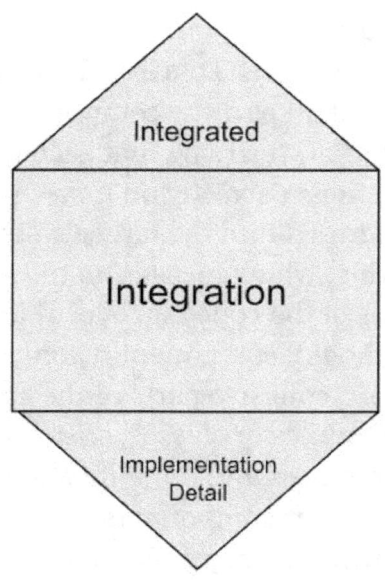

This model, also named "honeycomb," bears a strong resemblance to the Trophy model we discussed earlier. It focuses on providing fast and reliable feedback while covering all necessary aspects of microservices.

In this model, **Integrated Tests**, similar to the End-to-End tests discussed earlier, rely on the accuracy of other systems, making them unstable and less adaptable. Therefore, it's advisable not to invest heavily in these tests.

Implementation Detail Tests are more suitable for inherently isolated code sections with internal complexity. They focus on specific scenarios, such as log parsing, verifying that these isolated components perform as expected.

Lastly, **Integration Tests** in this context aim to verify a service's correctness in a more isolated manner, emphasizing explicit interaction points. This is where we should concentrate our test efforts.

Understanding and implementing a balanced approach to test automation is important for enhancing the efficiency of the testing process. By strategically applying models such as the Agile Testing Pyramid, Testing Trophy, and Honeycomb, quality engineering professionals can navigate the complexities of modern software development more effectively. This not only accelerates testing cycles but also supports the delivery of high-quality, reliable applications by fostering a comprehensive understanding of various testing strategies and their appropriate applications.

Advantages of QA Techniques

To end this section about QA techniques, let's highlight the main advantages of employing robust QA techniques, which are manifold and contribute significantly to the overall success of software projects. These techniques, whether manual or automated, offer several key benefits:

1. **Enhanced Product Quality.** Properly incorporating QE techniques into the Software Development Lifecycle (SDLC) helps identify and rectify defects early in the development process, whether through manual or automated methods. This integration leads to higher software quality and improved user satisfaction.
2. **Risk Mitigation.** By systematically testing software functionalities, QA techniques mitigate the risks associated with software failures, performance issues, and security vulnerabilities.
3. **Cost Efficiency.** Automated testing reduces manual effort, accelerates testing cycles, and optimizes resource allocation, thereby lowering overall testing costs and improving ROI.
4. **Continuous Improvement.** QA techniques facilitate continuous feedback and iterative improvements, enabling teams to refine software features, address user feedback, and adapt to changing market demands efficiently.

In conclusion, the effective application of Quality Assurance techniques, both manual and automated, is essential for helping to ensure the delivery of high-quality software products that meet user expectations and business requirements. By incorporating these techniques into the software development lifecycle, organizations can enhance reliability, boost efficiency, and foster innovation while maintaining a competitive edge in the market.

DEVOPS IN QUALITY ENGINEERING

DevOps represents a transformative approach to software development that emphasizes collaboration, automation, and continuous improvement across development, quality assurance (QA), and operations teams. DevOps frameworks aim to optimize workflows, boost productivity, and effectively deliver high-quality software products through Quality Engineering (QE) practices.

Continuous Integration and Continuous Delivery/Deployment (CI/CD)

A central tenet of DevOps in QE is the adoption of CI/CD pipelines, which automate the integration of new code changes, rigorously test them, and seamlessly deploy them into production environments. By automating these workflows, CI/CD pipelines ensure that software updates undergo comprehensive testing before release, reducing the risk of defects and improving overall software quality. This automation also accelerates delivery times, helping to enable teams to deliver updates to end-users swiftly and reliably.

Automation

Automation is pivotal in DevOps practices within Quality Engineering (QE), aiming to minimize manual effort and maintain consistency across testing, deployment, and monitoring processes. QE teams leverage automation tools and frameworks to streamline a wide array of tasks, including test data preparation, test results analysis, metrics gathering, and testing environment setup, alongside traditional test automation such as regression and performance testing. By adopting this comprehensive automation approach, QE professionals not only increase efficiency but also foster a more reliable and scalable software development environment. This optimization of resource utilization significantly reduces time-to-market for software releases.

Monitoring and Feedback

DevOps in QE emphasizes continuous monitoring of applications in production environments to gather real-time insights into performance metrics, system health, and user experience. Monitoring tools provide QE teams with actionable feedback on application behavior and identify potential issues or bottlenecks promptly. By proactively monitoring application performance, QE professionals can address emerging issues swiftly, optimize system performance, and enhance overall software reliability.

Collaboration and Communication

DevOps, akin to Agile methodologies, nurtures a collaborative culture among diverse teams comprising developers, testers, operations engineers, and stakeholders. QE professionals engage proactively in collaborative endeavors to establish quality goals, devise testing strategies, and prioritize enhancements throughout the software development lifecycle. This proactive communication promotes that quality is a collective responsibility, fostering transparency and optimizing the effectiveness of DevOps practices in delivering top-tier software products.

Integration of Agile and DevOps Practices

By integrating Agile and DevOps practices, QE teams leverage synergies between iterative development, continuous integration, automation, and collaborative workflows. This integration enhances team efficiency, accelerates delivery cycles, and facilitates rapid adaptation to changing requirements or market demands. QE professionals benefit from streamlined processes, enhanced visibility into project status, and the ability to deliver value to end-users more effectively.

DevOps has emerged as a pivotal framework for integrating development, QA, and operations within software engineering practices. By embracing CI/CD pipelines, automation, continuous monitoring, and fostering collaboration, DevOps in QE enables organizations to achieve faster delivery times, higher software quality, and improved responsiveness to customer needs. As QE professionals continue to evolve their practices within DevOps frameworks, they play a pivotal role in fostering innovation, optimizing workflows, and delivering exceptional software products that meet the highest standards of quality and reliability.

CONTINUOUS TESTING

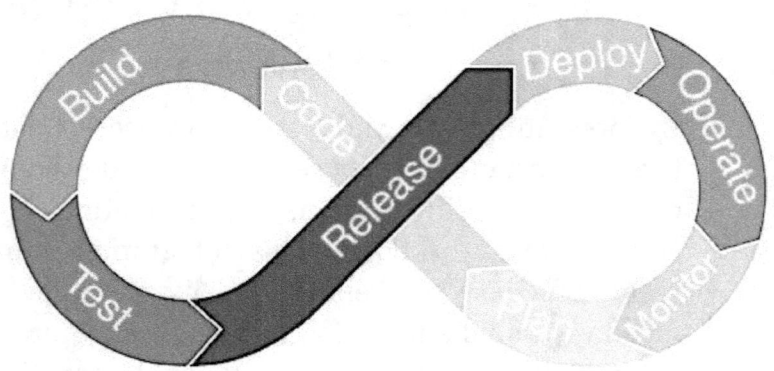

Continuous Testing is an integral part of modern Quality Engineering (QE) practices that integrates automated testing into the CI/CD pipeline. This approach ensures that software is continuously tested throughout its development lifecycle, from code integration to deployment, enabling rapid feedback and quality assurance.

Key Aspects of Continuous Testing

1. **Integration with CI/CD Pipeline.** Continuous Testing effortlessly embeds automated tests within the CI/CD pipeline, executing tests automatically every time new code changes are made. This helps ensure that every code commit undergoes testing, reducing the likelihood of defects reaching production.
2. **Immediate Feedback.** Automated tests provide immediate feedback on the quality of code changes. Developers receive instant notifications about test results, enabling them to quickly identify and address defects while the code is still fresh in their minds. This rapid feedback loop accelerates the development process and improves overall code quality.
3. **Risk Mitigation.** Continuous Testing is essential for early risk identification and mitigation within the development cycle. By detecting issues promptly, QE teams can proactively address potential risks, including security vulnerabilities, compatibility issues across different environments, and performance bottlenecks.

4. **Improved Collaboration.** Continuous Testing fosters collaboration among development, QA, and operations teams. By integrating automated testing processes into the CI/CD workflow, teams can work together more effectively. This integration ensures that everyone shares responsibility for quality and enhances communication through constant feedback loops.
5. **Faster Delivery.** By automating and accelerating the testing process, Continuous Testing enables faster delivery of software updates and releases. Rapid feedback and early defect detection streamline the deployment pipeline, allowing organizations to deliver high-quality software to users promptly and reliably.

Benefits of Continuous Testing

- **Efficiency and Productivity.** Automated tests reduce manual effort and repetitive tasks, allowing QE resources to concentrate on more strategic testing activities and innovation.
- **Agility and Adaptability.** Continuous Testing supports agile methodologies by facilitating continuous integration, delivery, and deployment of software updates, allowing organizations to swiftly adapt to market changes and customer feedback.
- **Customer Satisfaction and Business Impact.** Ultimately, Continuous Testing

contributes to improved customer satisfaction by delivering reliable, high-quality software products. By striving to meet user expectations and making sure software performs as intended, organizations can enhance their reputation, retain customers, and drive business growth. Continuous Testing aligns technical excellence with business objectives, enabling organizations to innovate confidently and stay competitive in dynamic markets.

Continuous Testing is essential for modern software development practices, providing immediate feedback, mitigating risks, fostering collaboration, and accelerating software delivery. By incorporating Continuous Testing into their QA strategies alongside manual and automated testing, Quality Engineers can help to introduce robust quality assurance processes that drive continuous improvement and successful software outcomes.

PERSONAL STORY: TRANSITIONING FROM THE ICE-CREAM CONE TO A BALANCED TESTING APPROACH

In my journey as a Quality Engineering Manager at various companies, one of the most common issues I've encountered is the reliance on the inverted pyramid, also known as the Ice Cream Cone test automation antipattern, developed by Alastair Scott and other engineers at ThoughtWorks in 2011.

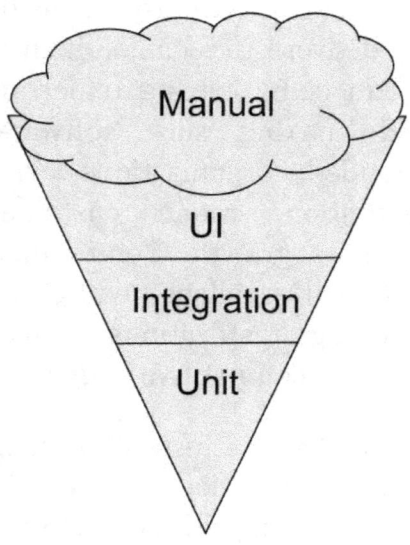

This model, heavily reliant on manual testing and UI-heavy automation, often leads to scalability challenges and inefficiencies. Here's a story from my experience that illustrates this problem and how adopting a balanced approach can significantly improve test efficiency and product quality.

The Ice-Cream Cone Model Challenge

When I joined one of the teams, I noticed that their test automation strategy was heavily focused on UI end-to-end tests. This made sense initially, as the Quality Engineers were transitioning from manual testing to partial automation. They started by automating the tests they ran daily, which were predominantly UI tests. Initially, they had a lot of long, flaky UI end-to-end tests because they were automating the same scenarios they used to run manually.

One of the problems I usually see in different projects is that after introducing Test Automation, QA teams proceed with writing test cases in the same way they have done before, without any changes. Eventually, the team realized that these tests were flaky and hard to maintain since they often failed before reaching the part they were supposed to test. In response, they swung to the opposite extreme, getting rid of all long end-to-end scenarios and breaking them into independent atomic tests focused on one functionality at a time. However, this extreme approach soon revealed its limitations.

Despite having thousands of automated UI tests, the team still missed critical bugs. One such incident occurred when a bug was introduced during a code refactor. This bug added an additional fee to the total price when users added items to their cart through the UI, causing significant overcharges. The QE team had designed separate automated tests for searching, cart, checkout, and reporting functionalities, all of which were fast and independent. However, none of these tests caught the bug because they were siloed and did not include an end-to-end scenario that verified the price consistency across different steps of the purchasing flow.

Shifting to a Balanced Approach

Recognizing the flaws in the ice-cream cone model, I advocated for a more balanced approach to test automation. We explored alternative frameworks such as the Testing Pyramid, Honeycomb, and the Testing Trophy, which emphasize a higher proportion of unit and integration tests over UI tests. This shift was not just an option but a necessity to keep our quality engineering efforts in step with our evolving product landscape.

Implementing the Change

Revisiting Test Cases. We started by revisiting and revising our test cases. QEs were encouraged to think critically about what really needed to be tested in each case and what could be simplified. For instance, instead of duplicating steps to search for an item, we streamlined the process by generating orders directly and testing the cart functionality.

Automated Visual Testing. We introduced automated visual testing tools to handle UI validation, which helped us separate concerns and keep our functional tests focused and manageable.

Granular Integration Tests. We increased our focus on integration tests that were fast and covered small, specific functionalities. These tests provided quick feedback and ensured that components interact correctly with each other.

End-to-End Testing Balance. While the majority of our tests were unit and integration tests, we still included a few critical end-to-end tests to cover scenarios like the one that caused the overcharging bug. This provided a safety net without overwhelming the automation suite with slow and brittle tests.

Trustworthy Tests. One major cultural change was addressing the reliability of our tests. We eliminated or fixed flaky tests to restore trust in our CI system. By ensuring that a red CI run indicated a real issue, we fostered a culture where failing tests were taken seriously and promptly addressed.

The Outcome

By transitioning from the ice-cream cone model to a more balanced approach, we achieved several benefits:

- Improved Efficiency. The new test automation strategy was more efficient, with faster test execution times and reduced maintenance efforts.
- Enhanced Test Coverage. We had better coverage of critical functionalities without the noise of unnecessary validations.
- Higher-Quality Products. Ultimately, this approach led to the delivery of higher-quality products to our customers, as we were able to catch and address issues earlier in the development process.

This experience reinforced the importance of continuously evaluating and adapting our testing and automation strategies to align with the growing complexity and needs of our products. Embracing frameworks like the Testing Pyramid, Honeycomb, and the Testing Trophy enabled us to build a more resilient and scalable test automation suite, allowing our quality engineering efforts to keep pace with our evolving product landscape.

CHAPTER 3

CHALLENGES AND SOLUTIONS IN QUALITY ENGINEERING

Navigating change management in the context of Quality Engineering (QE) involves handling the complexities and dynamics associated with evolving processes, technologies, and methodologies. As organizations strive to improve their quality assurance practices, managing these changes effectively becomes crucial to maintaining and enhancing software quality.

EMBRACING THE SHIFT LEFT PARADIGM

The Shift Left approach, which integrates testing and quality assurance activities early in the development cycle, represents a significant change in traditional software development practices. It requires a cultural shift, encouraging collaboration between developers, testers, and other stakeholders from the outset.

A 5-Step Transformation Process for Cultivating a Quality Culture

To successfully implement the Shift Left approach in Quality Engineering (QE), a deliberate strategy is essential. By embedding QE practices early in the software development lifecycle, organizations can proactively identify and address potential issues, enhancing software quality and accelerating time-to-market. Based on my experience, the following steps help cultivate a culture of quality ownership more effectively and rapidly:

1. **Eliminate Technical Debt.** Begin by addressing existing defects and accumulated technical debt. You can't start any transformation with a full "baggage" of defects. Neglecting accumulated technical debt and defects can lead to a backlog of unresolved unit tests and issues, impacting both release schedules and team morale.
2. **Build a Centralized Team of Quality and Test Automation Excellence.** Establish a specialized team dedicated to developing tools, building infrastructure, and creating effective automated tests. This team plays a crucial role in supporting developers to own their quality responsibilities. By centralizing expertise and resources, the team can:
   a. Create and maintain robust testing tools and frameworks that can be utilized across different projects, promoting consistency and efficiency in testing practices.
   b. Set up and manage scalable test environments that can handle the demands of CI/CD pipelines, enabling faster and more reliable testing cycles.
   c. Offer training sessions and ongoing support to developers and other team members, helping them understand and adopt good practices in test automation and quality assurance.

d. Encourage collaboration between developers, testers, and other stakeholders by establishing a platform for exchanging knowledge, tools, and techniques. This helps prevent redundant efforts and promotes a unified approach to quality.

By centralizing these activities, organizations can prevent redundant efforts, overcome common challenges, and establish a more streamlined and effective approach to quality engineering. This centralized team acts as a center of excellence, driving innovation and consistency in QE practices across the organization.

3. **Create Trainings/Workshops for Developers.** Educating and training all team members on the principles and benefits of Shift Left is essential for successful implementation. Training initiatives should focus on introducing new testing techniques, automation tools, and collaborative practices to the entire team. This helps developers, testers, product managers, and other stakeholders understand their roles in achieving early quality assurance goals. By fostering a shared understanding of Shift Left principles, teams can collaborate more effectively to integrate testing seamlessly into iterative development cycles. Training

programs also empower team members to leverage automation tools effectively, enhancing efficiency and reducing manual testing efforts. Provide resources on testing good practices from the planning and architecture phases of the software development lifecycle. Promote Behavior-Driven Development (BDD), Test-Driven Development (TDD), and Acceptance Test-Driven Development (ATDD) where applicable.

Note: BDD is a powerful approach, and in the right hands, it can save your project a lot of money and make your customers happy. However, BDD can be hard to adopt since it requires changes to many processes. In cases where BDD is considered overkill, I have seen ATDD work just fine, helping to bridge the gap between business requirements and implementation.

4. **Set and Track the Metrics That Matter Most.** Use data and metrics to monitor progress in the right direction. Everyone on the team should understand their testing landscape, including code and test coverage. This chapter will explore quality metrics further.

5. **Focus on User Experience Data and Customer Feedback Analysis.** Quality Engineers (QEs) who are embedded within product development teams, rather than part

of the centralized team, should focus on data-driven testing and customer feedback. This includes analyzing requirements, understanding customer issues, and collaborating with support teams, designers, and product managers. This approach promotes continuous process improvement and helps ensure optimal product quality. Early engagement of QEs in the project lifecycle is critical to anticipating quality risks and establishing effective testing strategies. By participating in project discussions, QEs help align quality goals with overall project objectives, ensuring that testing efforts are strategically aligned with business priorities. Their early involvement facilitates proactive measures to mitigate risks, prevent defects, and optimize the development process from inception.

Implementing these steps empowers teams to take ownership of quality tasks, with clear expectations for planning, testability, and maintainability. This proactive approach not only improves software quality by preventing defects early but also fosters a mindset of continuous improvement within the organization. By embedding QE practices into the early stages of development, organizations can achieve significant benefits, including reduced costs, faster time-to-market, and increased customer satisfaction.

Embracing Shift Left as a core principle enables teams to deliver high-quality software that meets the ever-changing demands of today's competitive landscape. This transformation requires equipping teams with the right tools and practices, engaging team members in the test automation process, and cultivating a culture of quality ownership. Achieving this level of quality ownership involves not just technical changes, but a fundamental shift in mindset and behavior across the organization. To illustrate the challenges and strategies for navigating such transformative change, we will next consider the "Three Fables of Change Management".

Three Fables of Change Management

Research indicates that a mere 9% of individuals who make New Year's resolutions successfully achieve them. Alarmingly, 23% abandon their resolutions by the end of the first week, and 43% give up by the end of January (Drive Research, 2023). These numbers resonate with me. Every January, I've noticed our local gym getting crowded with fresh New Year's resolutioners. I was one of them a couple of years ago, and by February, things usually go back to normal.

Anyone who has attempted to kick a bad habit, begin an exercise routine, or acquire a new skill understands that change is difficult for everyone. As humans, we are naturally inclined to favor routine. Anything that disrupts established patterns encounters significant resistance, especially when it involves transforming the way people work. Organizational change is tough, with many initiatives falling short. These failures often lead to substantial financial losses for companies. Harvard Business Review reports that around 70% of change initiatives fail (Harvard Business Review, 2000). The Corporate Executive Board Corporate Leadership Council study echoes this, stating that only one-third of such initiatives fully meet the organization's set goals (CEB Corporate Leadership Council, 2021). Horrifying, right? And there's more. A recent study by Willis Towers Watson found that only 43% of employees believe their organization is effective at managing change (WTW, 2023). According to a Gartner study, while 74% of leaders assert that they involved employees in creating a change strategy, only 42% of employees feel that they were actually included in this process (Gartner, 2023). This lack of engagement means employees often do not feel involved in what is going on, posing a real challenge for change initiatives.

Let's explore why so much negativity surrounds transformations at work. "The Frog in the Well" fable provides a hint about the biggest enemy of any change.

Once upon a time, there was a frog that lived at the bottom of a deep, dark well. The well was the only world the frog knew, and it believed that its well was the entire universe. The frog felt content and secure in its familiar surroundings. One day, a curious frog from a nearby pond visited the well. Excitedly, the well frog greeted its visitor and began boasting about how fortunate it was to live in such a safe and cozy place. The pond frog listened patiently and then shared tales of the vast pond and the open skies beyond. The well frog, however, dismissed these stories, convinced that its well was the best and safest place to be. Undeterred, the pond frog invited the well frog to come and see the pond for itself. The well frog hesitated, fearing the unknown. It worried about leaving the well's comfort and the potential dangers beyond. Eventually, the pond frog hopped away, leaving the well frog to continue its life in the limited space of the well.

The moral of the story is that those who resist change and remain in their comfort zones may miss out on broader perspectives and opportunities. It encourages openness to new experiences and a willingness to embrace change for personal growth. When individuals or groups within an organization resist or oppose proposed changes, it can hinder progress and create obstacles. This resistance may stem from various factors, including fear of the unknown, comfort with the status quo, or concerns about potential negative impacts. The psychological tendency known as loss aversion, where individuals emphasize avoiding losses more than acquiring equivalent gains, exacerbates this resistance. At work, this loss aversion is particularly high because it's about your job—the thing that supplies you with basic human needs like safety and security. Risking that for a slightly more productive work environment doesn't seem like a good gamble for our brains.

Think back to the last time someone tried to implement a new process or structure in your team. More than likely, you saw it as an extra burden. You were already busy without it, and this just added to your stress. So what did you do? If you're like most people, the second that initiative got behind schedule or didn't work out exactly as promised, you disengaged from it.

The second fable is called "Stone Soup."

Once upon a time, in a small village, a traveler passed through. Tired from his journey and hungry, he had nothing to eat. The traveler approached the villagers and asked for some food, but they were unwilling to share their supplies with anyone. Then the traveler took out a large, empty pot from his backpack, placed it in the center of the village square, filled it with water, set it over a fire, and dropped a simple stone into the pot. As the water began to boil, the traveler tasted it and exclaimed, "Ah, what a delicious stone soup this will be! But it would be even better with a few ingredients." One villager asked, "What kind of ingredients do you need?" The traveler replied, "Well, a few carrots would be nice." The villager decided to contribute a few carrots and added them to the pot. Another villager added a potato. This continued as more villagers contributed various vegetables, herbs, and spices to enhance the soup's taste. Soon, the once-empty pot was filled with a delicious soup, thanks to the contributions of the villagers. Finally, the entire village gathered around the pot, and they all enjoyed a feast together. The traveler and his "stone soup" had turned the villagers' selfishness into a spirit of sharing and community.

The fable highlights the power of engaging others and bringing them together. Ineffective communication and collaboration, among other factors, can lead to a lack of engagement, which is harmful to any organizational change. Think back to times when changes were implemented without your knowledge; it's never a pleasant experience.

I can definitely relate to that. At one of the previous companies I worked for, we underwent five reorganizations, including two rounds of layoffs, within three years. The constant changes left employees exhausted, demotivated, and fearful. When communication is lacking, gaining buy-in from team members becomes challenging. Sometimes, even securing buy-in for upcoming changes may not be enough. Ideally, team members should be actively involved in the change process—they should feel engaged.

The final fable I want to share with you is called "The Sun and the Wind".

Once upon a time, the Sun and the Wind engaged in a friendly competition to determine who was stronger. They wanted to see who could make a traveler take off his coat. The Wind went first, blowing with all its might, trying to forcibly remove the traveler's coat.

However, the more the Wind blew, the tighter the traveler held onto his coat. Eventually, the Wind grew tired and admitted defeat. Next, it was the Sun's turn. The Sun smiled warmly and gently sent its rays down to the Earth. As the traveler felt the Sun's warmth, he started to feel hot in his coat. Gradually, he realized that the coat was unnecessary. So, he willingly took off his coat and enjoyed the pleasant warmth.

The moral of the fable is that there are different ways or strategies to make change happen. Even with abundant resources and power, the wrong strategy and leadership can hinder the success of change. Successful organizational transformation relies on strong leadership that offers clear guidance, support, and resources throughout the process. Without a well-defined, transparent change strategy, even ample resources may not prevent failure.

Now that we've identified the main obstacles to change, it's time to explore how to overcome them. This is where Kotter's 8-Step Change Model becomes invaluable. Kotter (1996) outlines a systematic and effective approach to implementing change within an organization in his book *Leading Change*. Having applied this framework numerous times, I can attest to its efficacy. Kotter outlines eight crucial steps that organizations need to follow in order to effectively tackle challenges and implement significant transformations.

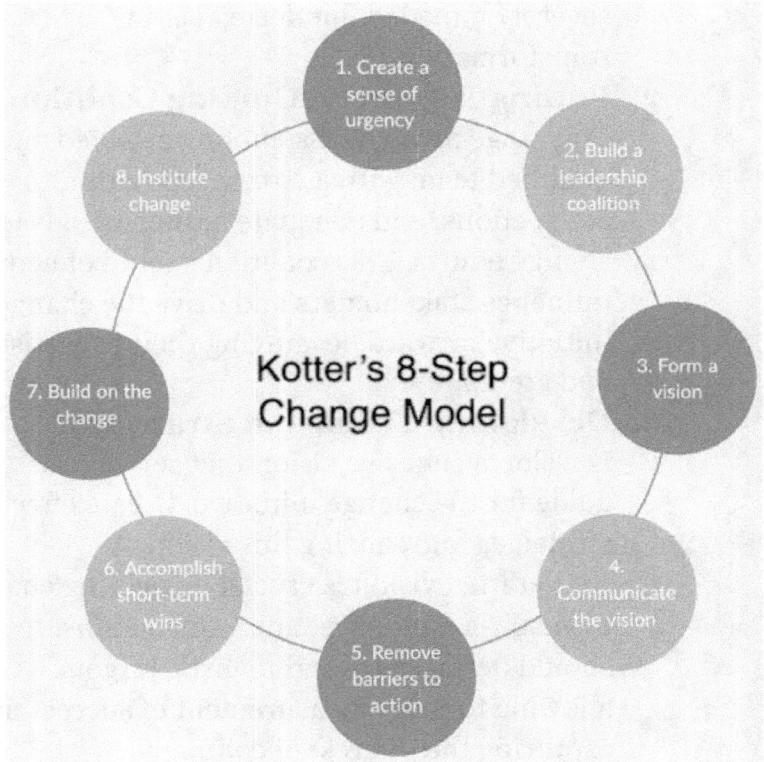

By following these steps, the organization will be more likely to embrace and commit to the changes by the end of the process.

1. **Creating a Sense of Urgency.** Initiating the process requires fostering a sense of urgency among all employees, including managers. It is crucial for everyone involved to recognize the necessity for change and understand its significance for organizational growth. Without this shared urgency, the momentum of the change initiative can be

severely impeded, hindering lasting transformation.

2. **Putting Together a Guiding Coalition.** This stage involves assembling a skilled and qualified team with a strong reputation, connections, and adequate authority to lead change efforts. This coalition should effectively influence stakeholders and drive the change initiative forward, leveraging their expertise and credibility.

3. **Developing Vision and Strategies.** Develop a cohesive vision that serves as a guide for the change initiative. Create effective strategies for realizing this vision. A well-crafted vision is crucial in steering change by inspiring and directing team actions. It should define clear and realistic targets, allowing for easy measurement of success and capturing the interest of company stakeholders.

4. **Communicating the Change Vision.** Skillfully convey the vision and strategies to encourage widespread acceptance and support for the change initiative within the organization. The goal is to capture the hearts and minds of employees, motivating them to support the change. Emphasize the benefits of the change for both the organization and the individuals involved.

5. **Removing Barriers to Action.** Identify and eliminate obstacles that hinder progress.

These obstacles can take various forms, such as inadequate processes, employee resistance, disempowered managers, and structural challenges. The guiding coalition and senior management should focus on removing these barriers to facilitate smooth implementation of the change vision.

6. **Accomplishing Short-Term Wins.** Set and celebrate early, visible, and relevant goals, known as quick wins. These short-term achievements help sustain momentum, build confidence, and foster continued support for the change initiative. Prolonged periods without milestones can demoralize employees, so establishing and celebrating these quick wins is crucial.

7. **Building on the Change.** Maintain the execution of change by having teams consistently work towards the vision while monitoring progress. Avoid declaring victory prematurely after a few successes. Analyze each win to identify what worked and areas for improvement, keeping the momentum of change going.

8. **Making Change Stick.** Embed the change into the organizational culture by aligning norms, values, processes, and reward systems with the new direction. This phase involves establishing a supportive infrastructure that solidifies the change as a permanent part of the organization's operations.

By adhering to these eight steps, you can effectively guide the implementation of change within your organization, fostering a committed and proactive environment that embraces transformation and drives sustained growth. Each step, from creating a sense of urgency to embedding change in the organizational culture, is designed to address common challenges and establish a solid foundation for enduring success.

Let's summarize what we have just learned. Organizational transformations can be tough, with plenty of hurdles that might trip you up. The usual suspects? Resistance to change, apathy, and misguidance. These challenges can stall progress and dampen enthusiasm, but here's the secret sauce: Kotter's 8-Step Change Model. It's your trusty sidekick for navigating and conquering these obstacles, ensuring that your transformation efforts are both effective and sustainable. This model equips you with the strategies needed to drive meaningful change and achieve lasting growth.

As a bonus, I've attached a Stone Soup recipe.

Add the stone.

Peel and cut up carrots, potatoes, onions, and celery.

Boil these ingredients until soft.

Add tomatoes, corn, peas, and bouillon.

Add salt and boil for 10 minutes.

Remove the stone.

Serve with crackers.

Cook it with your team and enjoy!

Change is hard, but it is an integral part of growth—both for individuals and companies. Standing still for too long guarantees you'll be left in the dust.

QUALITY METRICS AS YOUR COMPASS

It's often said that "what gets measured, gets managed", a concept popularized by Peter Drucker. Indeed, metrics serve as our compass, helping us navigate the complex landscape of change with clarity and precision. As organizations embrace Shift left transformation, they face a fundamental challenge: how to measure the success of 'shift left' and its impact on product quality.

The absence of effective quality-related metrics poses a significant obstacle. Without a structured system to quantify the outcomes of 'shift left,' organizations are left in the dark, unable to gauge the effectiveness of their efforts, identify areas for improvement, or justify resource allocation. This problem highlights the critical need for a set of well-defined quality metrics that can serve as the compass for organizations embarking on 'shift left' transformations. The absence of such metrics hinders the ability to measure the success of 'shift left,' making it impossible to navigate the path to higher software quality and the benefits it promises to deliver.

Now let's dive into some quality metrics that we could measure to track the quality of our products:

Customer Satisfaction

Marshall Field once said, "Right or wrong, the customer is always right." This principle underscores the importance of prioritizing customer satisfaction as the ultimate goal in any business endeavor. No matter how technically sound a product may be—with 100% code coverage, 10,000 automated tests, and zero defects in the backlog—these metrics are meaningless if the customers are not satisfied. The true measure of a product's quality is defined by its users, and their feedback is invaluable for guiding improvements and ensuring that the product meets their needs and expectations.

To assess customer satisfaction effectively, gathering feedback from customers or end-users is essential. This can be achieved through various methods such as surveys, feedback forms, and direct interactions.

Monitoring app store reviews for native apps provides real-time insights into customer opinions and experiences. Additionally, conducting A/B testing allows you to compare different versions of a product to determine which one resonates more with users. Usability testing sessions, where real users interact with the product while observers take notes, are also critical for identifying pain points and areas for improvement. By actively seeking and analyzing customer feedback, you can make informed decisions that enhance the user experience, drive product improvements, and ultimately help to ensure that your customers remain satisfied and loyal.

Escaped Defects and Customer-Reported Complaints

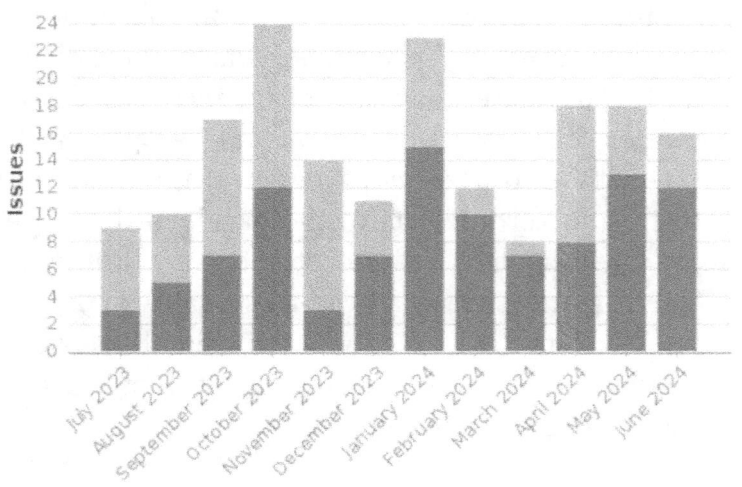

The dark gray portion of the bar represents defects reported by the internal team, while the light gray indicates customer-reported complaints. The peaks in complaints during October and April could suggest that features released in these months were controversial for users.

Working closely with your support team to identify the primary concerns raised by customers is crucial for maintaining and improving product quality. Collaborating with support staff allows you to gain direct access to the issues customers encounter, providing a wealth of real-world data that can be invaluable for identifying defects and usability problems. Tracking customer-reported issues or support tickets systematically contributes to capturing a comprehensive view of the product's performance from the user's perspective. This approach not only highlights the most pressing defects that need immediate attention but also reveals patterns and recurring problems that might indicate deeper underlying issues. By addressing these concerns promptly and effectively, you can enhance customer satisfaction and prevent minor issues from escalating into major problems.

Moreover, tracking and analyzing customer-reported issues helps prioritize which defects need to be addressed first and guides improvements in your testing and code coverage. Implementing labels or tags in your bug tracking system for user-reported issues makes it easier to categorize and retrieve these reports, ensuring that no critical feedback is overlooked. This organized approach enables development and QA teams to focus on areas that significantly impact the user experience, thereby optimizing their efforts and resources. Additionally, this process provides valuable insights into potential gaps in your testing strategy, allowing you to refine and expand your test cases to cover scenarios that may have been previously missed. By continuously learning from customer feedback and iteratively improving your product, you can build a more resilient and user-friendly application that meets and exceeds customer expectations.

Created/Resolved Defects Trend

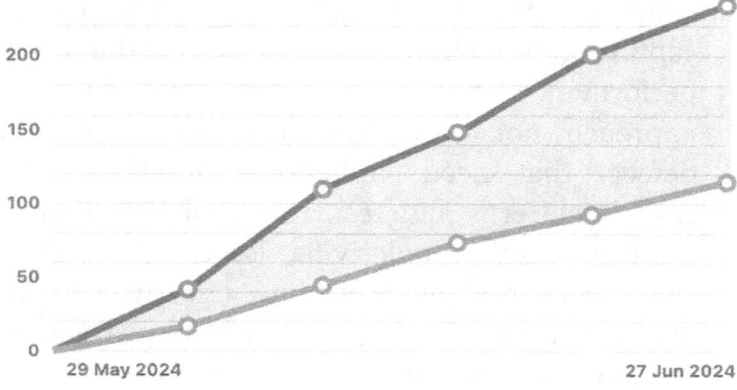

This graph indicates a concerning trend, as approximately 100 unresolved defects (220 created minus 120 resolved) have been added to the backlog over the month.

Created/Resolved defects is one of the basic metrics everyone should keep an eye on:

(Number of Created Bugs – Number of Resolved Bugs) over time

If the number of unresolved defects is increasing, it could pose a significant risk to the project. Waiting until the final stages of development to address these issues may not leave enough time for proper fixes and verification, potentially compromising the quality of the release. Instead, it's crucial to aim to address and resolve defects within each sprint, maintaining an agile and responsive development process. If you observe a noticeable upward trend in the Created-vs-Resolved ratio, this could be an indicator of accumulating technical debt. In such cases, it's important to work with the product manager to create a separate user story focused on addressing these growing issues. Postponing fixes with the mindset of "We will release it now and fix it later" can be risky, as this 'later' often never arrives. Subsequent deadlines and priorities can cause these defects to accumulate, leading to unmanageable technical debt that can snowball out of control, ultimately affecting the product's stability and performance.

In situations where releasing a product with known defects is unavoidable, it is essential to revisit and triage the growing backlog of defects. This might involve allocating a special sprint dedicated solely to addressing these issues. Additionally, consider revisiting defects that were raised over six months ago. Some of these may need to be closed, acknowledging the reality that the resources or time to address them may never materialize. This process helps in maintaining a realistic and manageable backlog. Setting up and monitoring the Created/Resolved defects chart is straightforward, as it is one of the default charts in all major bug tracking systems. Monitoring this metric helps to keep technical debt under control, prevents the degradation of product quality over time, and helps maintain a balance between new feature development and necessary bug fixes. This proactive approach ultimately leads to more stable and reliable software releases, meeting user expectations and maintaining customer satisfaction.

Total Number of Defects Grouped by Root Cause

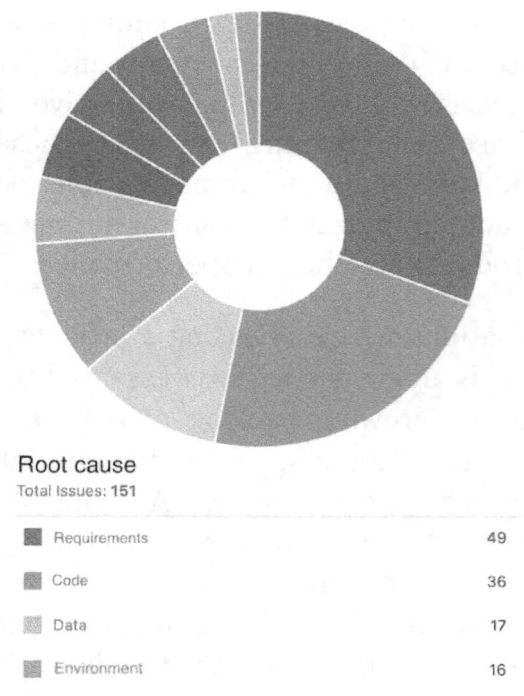

Root cause
Total Issues: 151

Requirements	49
Code	36
Data	17
Environment	16

This pie chart illustrates the distribution of defects grouped by their root causes, with the majority of issues stemming from requirements and coding. This highlights the need for focused quality improvement initiatives in these two critical areas.

When analyzing reported defects, it's crucial to identify their root causes. This process, although time-consuming, is invaluable as it uncovers the primary sources of bugs, which can include requirements, architecture, design, code, environment, or data. It's also a good practice to review defects and their root causes that have emerged during the last sprint in a retrospective meeting. This simple addition to the process helps to guarantee that we generate action items to address defects at their source.

Note: Based on my professional experience, the proportion of regression bugs should ideally not exceed 20% of the total number of bugs. This benchmark has proven effective in maintaining quality and efficiency in software development processes. This approach helps teams focus predominantly on bugs related to new features or changes in the software, rather than being overwhelmed by issues stemming from previous modifications.

Use existing or configure a new 'Root Cause' field in your bug tracking system. When closing a bug ticket after fixing a defect, remember to complete this field. The root cause might be one of the following:

- **Requirements**: If the defect is primarily due to misunderstandings or ambiguities in the project's requirements, consider whether the issue can be traced back to differences in

interpretation, missing requirements, or changes in project goals that weren't properly communicated. A root cause in this category often indicates a requirement-related problem.
- **Implementation (Code)**: Implementation-related defects are usually rooted in the codebase. If the defect is directly associated with syntax errors, logical flaws, or a lack of test coverage, it's likely an implementation issue. Pay attention to the code, tests, and code review process to identify this root cause.
- **Environment**: This category includes defects caused by external factors not directly controlled by the deployment process, such as server configurations, third-party integrations, or network settings that influence the runtime operation of the software.
- **Data**: This category deals with defects arising from data anomalies, incorrect data handling, integration issues, or problems related to data quality and consistency. Consider whether defects are related to poor data architecture, incorrect data input, errors in data processing or inadequate data validation procedures.
- **Deployment**: This category specifically addresses issues that arise during the deployment process itself, such as errors in deployment scripts, configuration issues during the deployment phase, or problems that occur when migrating software from a

development environment to production. Focus on the procedural aspects of how software is released and deployed.
- **Design**: For design-related defects, focus on whether the issue is fundamentally tied to architectural choices made during the project's design phase. If the defect's origin lies in the system's overall structure, technology selections, or the failure to address scalability or security, it likely falls under the design category.

By examining the defect in the context of these categories and identifying which one aligns most closely with the issue's origin, you can distinguish the root cause and categorize it accordingly in your tracking system. The 5-Whys framework is suggested to identify a root cause and not just a symptom. This data will help you create a pie chart or a two-dimensional table to identify the primary sources of your product's defects.

LEVERAGING AUTOMATION AND AI IN QUALITY ENGINEERING

The integration of automation and Artificial Intelligence (AI) into Quality Engineering (QE) practices marks a transformative shift in how software testing and quality assurance are approached. These advanced technologies offer capabilities that may significantly enhance efficiency, accuracy, and overall effectiveness in helping to ensure software quality.

Strategies for Integrating Automation and AI

1. **Identify Automation and AI Opportunities.** Initiating the integration of automation and AI begins with a comprehensive assessment of existing QE processes. This assessment aims to identify specific areas where automation can deliver the highest value. Typically, QE teams target repetitive and time-consuming tasks that are prime candidates for automation. Examples include regression testing, performance testing, and data validation processes. By automating these tasks, teams can reduce manual effort, accelerate testing cycles, and maintain consistent test execution across different environments and configurations. Moreover, there are numerous AI-driven tools available that help generate test cases and automate them with minimal supervision. I have always been against record and playback tools, but with machine learning algorithms under the hood, they have become very powerful and easy to maintain. These advanced tools analyze patterns, learn from past data, and adapt to changes in the

application, thereby significantly enhancing the efficiency and effectiveness of test automation efforts.
2. **Invest in Training.** Successful adoption of automation and AI technologies hinges on equipping Quality Engineers (QEs) with the requisite skills and knowledge. Investing in training programs focused on automation tools and AI-driven technologies is essential. Training should encompass not only technical proficiency in using these tools but also understanding their application within the QE framework. QEs should learn how to design, develop, and maintain automated test scripts, interpret AI-driven analytics for predictive testing, and integrate automation into CI/CD pipelines effectively. By empowering QEs with robust training, organizations enable them to leverage automation and AI to its fullest potential, thereby enhancing testing efficiency and accuracy.
3. **Gradual Implementation.** Transitioning to automation and AI should be approached incrementally to mitigate risks and minimize disruption to ongoing projects. Organizations typically begin with small-scale pilot projects or proof-of-concept initiatives. These initial implementations serve as test beds to validate the feasibility and benefits of automation and AI in real-world scenarios. Successful pilot projects provide empirical evidence of

improved test coverage, faster time-to-market, and reduced costs associated with manual testing efforts. As confidence and proficiency grow within the QE team, organizations can gradually expand automation initiatives across broader QE processes and projects.

By strategically implementing these strategies, organizations can harness the full potential of automation and AI in QE, driving continuous improvement in software quality and performance. Embracing these technologies not only enhances testing capabilities but also positions organizations to meet the ever-increasing demands for rapid and reliable software delivery in today's competitive landscape.

HIRING AND DEVELOPING QUALITY ENGINEERS

In today's rapidly evolving technological landscape, the demand for Quality Engineers (QEs) with DevOps and AI skills continues to rise, driven by the increasing complexity of software systems and the growing emphasis on delivering high-quality products to market quickly. As organizations strive to adopt agile methodologies, implement continuous integration and deployment practices, embrace digital transformation, and leverage AI, the role of

QEs has expanded far beyond traditional testing functions.

Expanding Role of Quality Engineers

Quality Engineers now play a pivotal role in helping to ensure software quality across the entire development lifecycle. Beyond executing test cases and identifying defects, QEs are instrumental in implementing automated testing frameworks, integrating quality practices early in the development process through Shift Left approaches, and collaborating effectively with cross-functional teams. Their responsibilities span from designing test strategies and frameworks to optimizing testing processes, all aimed at delivering robust, reliable, and user-centric software solutions.

Challenges in Hiring Quality Engineers

Despite the critical role QEs play, organizations face significant challenges in sourcing and retaining top talent.

1. **Talent Shortage.** The market faces a substantial shortage of skilled QEs who possess a blend of technical proficiency, domain knowledge, and cultural alignment with organizational values. This scarcity makes it challenging for companies to find suitable candidates capable of meeting the

dynamic demands of modern software development.
2. **Competition for Talent.** Intensifying competition among organizations further complicates the hiring landscape. To attract and retain top QEs, companies must offer competitive compensation packages, opportunities for career advancement, and an appealing work culture that prioritizes innovation, collaboration, and continuous learning.
3. **Evolving Skill Requirements.** The rapid evolution of technologies and methodologies necessitates that QEs continuously update their skills. Proficiency in automation tools, expertise in CI/CD pipelines, familiarity with cloud platforms, a solid grasp of agile principles, and knowledge of AI technologies are increasingly becoming prerequisites for the role. However, the ability to design and implement effective test strategies remains paramount. A QE's technical acumen must be complemented by a deep understanding of testing fundamentals to enable them to not only utilize the latest tools but also design tests that accurately assess product quality and user experience. Finding candidates who possess the right blend of technical expertise, the ability to design good tests, and a passion for their craft poses a persistent challenge for hiring managers

Strategies for Successful Hiring

To overcome the challenges of hiring quality engineers, organizations must adopt a strategic approach to talent acquisition. This includes:

1. **Define Clear Job Roles.** It's essential to clearly outline the roles and responsibilities of quality engineers within your organization, taking into account the specific needs of your projects and teams. While it's important to highlight the skills and foundational knowledge required, focusing too heavily on specific tools or programming languages can be limiting. Instead, emphasize the ability to learn and adapt to new technologies, as the underlying principles of good engineering are often transferable across different platforms. Explicitly communicate to potential candidates the core competencies and problem-solving skills they need to succeed in the role. Additionally, ensure you maintain a 'healthy' mix of seniority on your team. While it's beneficial to have many Senior and Staff Engineers, including more Junior roles is crucial. Junior team members can learn from their Senior counterparts and bring fresh, diverse ideas to the team.
2. **Prioritize Training and Development.** Continually offer training and development opportunities to enhance the skills of your

current team members and attract new talent. Offer certification programs, workshops, dev bootcamps, online courses and mentorship programs to foster continuous learning and growth.

3. **Emphasize Cultural Fit.** Look for candidates who not only possess the requisite technical skills but also align with the cultural values and ethos of your organization. Prioritize attributes such as collaboration, adaptability, and a passion for quality.

4. **Leverage Networking and Referrals.** Tap into professional networks, industry events, and online communities to identify potential candidates. Encourage employee referrals and offer incentives for successful hires.

5. **Offer Competitive Compensation and Benefits.** In a competitive market, offering competitive salaries, benefits, and perks can help attract top-quality engineers. Consider flexible work arrangements, professional development opportunities, and other incentives to retain talent.

6. **Incorporate AI Expertise.** As AI becomes more integral to modern software development, consider prioritizing candidates with skills in AI-driven tools, machine learning algorithms, and data analysis. Highlight AI proficiency in job descriptions and ensure training programs include AI-related skills. This strategy will enhance

your team's capabilities and position your organization at the forefront of technological advancements.

In summary, addressing the growing demand for QEs with DevOps and AI skills requires strategic recruitment practices that encompass defining clear job roles, emphasizing cultural fit, and leveraging effective networking channels. By proactively addressing these challenges and investing in talent acquisition strategies, organizations can build a resilient and proficient QE team capable of driving continuous improvement and delivering high-quality software solutions.

Developing Existing Quality Engineers

Investing in the continuous development of Quality Engineers (QEs) is imperative for organizations aiming to maintain high standards of software quality amidst rapid technological advancements and evolving industry practices. By nurturing the skills and expertise of existing team members, companies not only enhance their QE capabilities but also foster a culture of continuous improvement and innovation.

Strategies for Developing QEs

1. **Ongoing Training and Development.** Continuous learning is crucial for keeping Quality Engineers updated on the latest tools, methodologies, and industry trends.

Organizations should offer comprehensive training programs that cater to both technical skills and soft skills development. This includes workshops, seminars, online courses, and certification programs tailored to QE roles. By investing in their professional growth, organizations empower QEs to excel in their roles and contribute effectively to project success.

2. **Foster Cross-Functional Collaboration.** Facilitating collaboration among diverse teams and disciplines fosters an environment where Quality Engineers (QEs) interact with experts from various knowledge domains. By actively engaging in cross-functional teams, QEs gain invaluable insights spanning the entire software development lifecycle, encompassing phases from initial requirements gathering through to deployment and ongoing maintenance. This multifaceted involvement not only enriches their problem-solving capabilities but also hones their communication skills. Moreover, it fosters a comprehensive approach to quality assurance, where QEs integrate insights from different perspectives to promote robust software quality and alignment with project objectives.

3. **Stay Abreast of Emerging Technologies.** The QE landscape is continuously evolving with advancements in automation, AI-driven testing, cloud technologies, and agile

methodologies. Encourage QEs to stay updated on emerging technologies through industry publications, webinars, conferences, and participation in relevant communities. Providing access to resources and fostering a culture of innovation enables QEs to apply cutting-edge practices and tools effectively in their daily work.

Benefits of Developing QEs

Investing in the development of existing QEs yields several benefits for organizations:

- **Enhanced Expertise.** Skilled and knowledgeable QEs contribute to improved software quality, reduced defects, and enhanced user satisfaction.
- **Adaptability.** Well-trained QEs are equipped to adapt quickly to changes in technology and business requirements, allowing for agile responses to evolving project needs.
- **Team Collaboration.** Cross-functional collaboration fosters a cohesive team environment where QEs work synergistically with developers, product managers, and stakeholders.
- **Innovation.** QEs who are well-versed in emerging technologies drive innovation within the QE team, introducing efficient testing strategies and optimizing workflows.

By prioritizing the development of existing QEs through continuous training, cross-functional collaboration, and exposure to emerging technologies, organizations cultivate a skilled and adaptable QE workforce. This proactive approach not only addresses the challenges of talent shortages and skill gaps but also positions companies to produce high-quality software products that satisfy the needs of modern consumers and thrive in competitive markets. Investing in QE development is an investment in long-term success and sustainable growth in the digital age.

PERSONAL STORY: THE TRANSFORMATION CHALLENGE

Throughout my tenure as Head of Quality Engineering, I've gained numerous insights into implementing organizational change, especially the significance of monitoring metrics that gauge not only product quality but also team well-being and the efficiency of internal processes. One such lesson came during a transformation initiative that required several incremental changes, highlighting the crucial role of comprehensive metrics and active team involvement.

The Importance of Tracking Metrics During Transformations

A few years ago, I led a shift-left transformation in one of the world's well-known companies. The transformation aimed to integrate quality earlier into the development process, reducing bugs and improving overall product quality. I was confident that our changes would yield positive results, and we, as the QE department, diligently tracked metrics to demonstrate improvements. However, midway through the transformation, I received feedback from my team that hit me hard: "We have made a lot of changes without tracking the team's success metrics".

This feedback was a wake-up call. While we were focused on how the changes improved our product, we had overlooked metrics that assessed how these changes impacted the team itself. It became apparent that to succeed, we needed to track metrics related to internal processes and team morale. Preventing regression in these processes was as important as improving product quality.

The Importance of Involvement and Buy-In

One critical aspect of managing change is effective communication. Without it, gaining buy-in from team members becomes challenging. I realized that securing initial buy-in for upcoming changes was not enough; team members needed to be actively involved in the change process. They should feel engaged and part of the journey.

An example of my oversight occurred during another transformation. I used to have a tendency as a manager to share documents about team processes only when they were nearly finalized. I did this to achieve completeness and minimize rework, intending to demonstrate my capability to produce high-quality documentation. In one extreme instance seven years ago, while preparing for a major organizational transformation, I shared a 15-page document with the team just one week before presenting it to the entire company. My intention was positive—I wanted to spare the team from the burden of dealing with extensive documentation because, let's face it, documentation isn't the most exciting task.

Despite incorporating the team's feedback and getting their buy-in about the content ahead of time, the team did not receive the document enthusiastically. They felt somewhat excluded from the process, even though I had included information based on our discussions over the previous two months. It was clear that for a successful transformation, team members needed to be more than just recipients of information; they needed to be active contributors.

Implementing a Balanced Approach

To address these issues, I implemented several changes:

- Tracking Comprehensive Metrics. We started tracking metrics related to team performance and internal processes alongside product

quality metrics. This included tracking team morale, process efficiency, and feedback cycles.
- Early and Continuous Involvement. I began involving the team early in the documentation process, seeking their input and feedback from the outset. This approach made them feel engaged and valued, leading to better acceptance and smoother implementation of changes.
- Regular Check-Ins. We established regular check-ins to discuss ongoing changes, gather feedback, and adjust our strategies as needed. This iterative process helped maintain alignment and address any concerns promptly.

The Outcome

By adopting this balanced approach, we achieved several benefits:

- Improved Team Morale: The team felt more involved and valued, which boosted morale and engagement.
- Enhanced Process Efficiency: Tracking internal metrics helped us identify and address process inefficiencies, leading to smoother operations.

Leadership and Change Models

Successful organizational transformation relies on strong leadership that offers clear guidance, support, and resources throughout the process. Without a well-defined, transparent change strategy, even ample resources may not prevent failure. Two models that have been instrumental in understanding and managing change are the Scott and Jaffe Change Model and the Bridges Transition Model.

- **Scott and Jaffe Change Model**

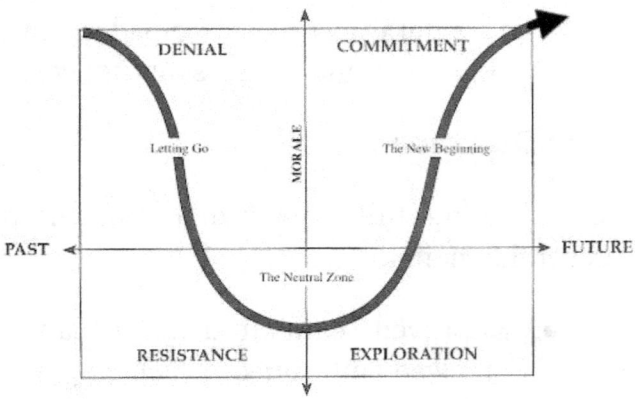

This model, introduced by Cynthia Scott and Dennis Jaffe in their article "Survive and Thrive in Times of Change.", outlines the stages people go through during change—Denial, Resistance, Exploration, and Commitment. It emphasizes that people transition at different speeds and may need guidance and support to move through these stages successfully.

- **Bridges Transition Model**

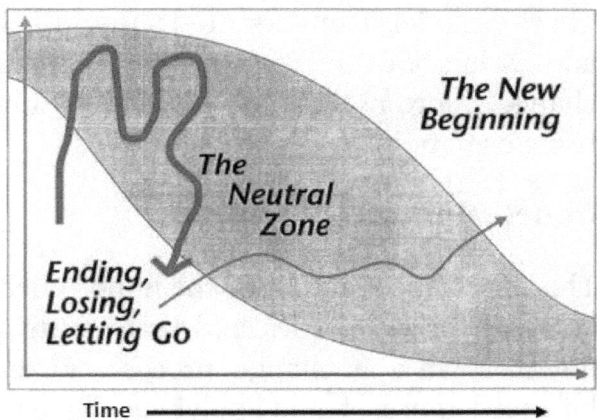

This model, developed by William Bridges and introduced in his 1991 book "Managing Transitions: Making the Most of Change", complements the Scott and Jaffe model by focusing on the emotional and psychological aspects of transitions during change. It emphasizes the importance of guiding individuals from the Ending, Losing, Letting Go phase, through the Neutral Zone, to the New Beginning.

The key concept here is that individuals in the Neutral Zone may cycle through phases of resistance and exploration before moving forward. There is also the risk that they might "give up" and return to "the old way" if that remains an option (represented by the bold curved line). The goal for any organizational change leader is to navigate the affected population through the transition from the current state to the desired future state as swiftly and smoothly as possible.

These models underscored the importance of addressing both the technical and human aspects of change, promoting a holistic approach to transformation.

Conclusion

This experience reinforced the importance of tracking comprehensive metrics and actively involving team members in the change process. By embracing a balanced approach and applying change management models, we were able to navigate the complexities of transformation, ensuring that our quality engineering efforts kept pace with our evolving product landscape.

CHAPTER 4

FUTURE TRENDS AND INNOVATIONS

As technology evolves at an exponential rate, the landscape of Quality Engineering (QE) is poised for significant transformation. The integration of cutting-edge technologies and innovative methodologies will redefine the roles and responsibilities of Quality Engineers, enabling them to elevate software quality to unprecedented levels with greater efficiency and agility.

THE IMPACT OF AI ON QUALITY ENGINEERING

Artificial Intelligence (AI) is revolutionizing Quality Engineering (QE) with cutting-edge technologies that streamline and enhance the entire testing and assurance process. These AI-driven innovations are setting the stage for more efficient, accurate, and dynamic QE practices.

Expanding Horizons in QE with AI

- **AI-Powered Test Case Generation.** AI is transforming the landscape of test case generation by applying machine learning algorithms to parse and understand large codebases and user data. This shift automates and expedites the creation of test cases, traditionally a manual and time-intensive endeavor. AI not only speeds up this process but also enhances the comprehensiveness of

test coverages, adapting to complex system architectures and simulating real-world user behaviors. This results in a more effective detection of potential flaws early in the development cycle, significantly improving the robustness of software products.
- **AI-Enhanced Visual Testing.** AI is revolutionizing visual testing by automating the verification of graphical user interfaces across different devices and resolutions. These AI-driven tools can quickly identify discrepancies in layout, color, size, and text that might be missed by human eyes, ensuring that the UI adheres to design specifications. By automating visual checks, AI reduces the time spent on manual reviews and increases the accuracy of detecting visual regressions, helping to maintain a consistent user experience across all platforms.
- **Predictive Analytics in Testing.** AI-enhanced predictive analytics are changing the way QE teams forecast and address potential software issues. Leveraging past data and predictive models, these tools can foresee likely problem areas and system failures, enabling teams to focus their testing efforts more strategically. This proactive approach allows for better resource allocation and test planning, addressing potential issues before they escalate, thus optimizing the overall testing process and efficiency.

- **Advanced Defect Management.** AI technologies enhance defect management by automating the detection, categorization, and prioritization of software bugs. These systems use sophisticated algorithms to analyze defects based on their severity, potential impact, and patterns observed over time, accelerating the resolution process while reducing the likelihood of significant disruptions. This intelligent defect management supports a continuous enhancement cycle within QE practices, offering actionable insights to refine testing strategies and boost software quality.
- **Enhanced Requirement Testing and Issue Detection.** AI tools also play a crucial role in the early stages of the software development lifecycle by scrutinizing requirements and specifications for clarity and consistency. They identify potential issues at the outset, aiding in the refinement of requirements and the prevention of downstream defects. This proactive vetting helps ensure that the final software products are of higher quality and align more closely with user needs and expectations.

AI's Role in the Future of QE

The integration of AI into QE is forging a path toward unprecedented efficiency and effectiveness in software testing and quality assurance. As AI technology continues to advance, it will further empower quality engineers to address more complex software challenges with greater agility and precision. This evolution is pivotal not only for enhancing product quality but also for maintaining a competitive edge in the rapidly evolving digital marketplace.

Embracing AI-driven approaches in QE is essential for organizations aiming to lead in technological innovation and to excel in delivering superior software solutions that meet the stringent demands of modern users and markets.

Challenges and Considerations in Adopting AI for Quality Engineering

Although AI significantly enhances Quality Engineering, it introduces specific challenges. AI models depend heavily on extensive, high-quality data for training. Insufficient or low-quality data can generate models that inadvertently encode biases, perpetuating these in automated processes. The complexity of AI algorithms can result in a lack of transparency, making it difficult for teams to understand and trust AI-driven decisions. This "black box" nature of AI can complicate debugging and accountability when errors occur. Moreover, the deployment and continuous refinement of AI frameworks demand substantial resources, necessitating considerable investment in technology and specialized expertise. Organizations must therefore adopt a thorough approach to AI adoption, incorporating exhaustive testing, precise validation, and stringent ethical guidelines to address these risks effectively. Ethical considerations will be explored further later in this chapter.

THE ROLE OF QUALITY ENGINEERS AS ENABLERS

The future trajectory of Quality Engineering (QE) hinges on the seamless integration of DevOps methodologies and continuous testing practices, marking a pivotal shift towards collaborative, automated, and feedback-driven software development processes.

Quality Engineers' Mission in These New Realities

In the new Shift Left reality, where everyone shares responsibility for quality, Quality Engineers (QEs) play a crucial role in orchestrating and championing a culture of quality throughout the software development lifecycle. While the entire team shares responsibility for delivering a high-quality product, QEs contribute unique skills and perspectives essential for maintaining a robust quality process. Here are some key responsibilities for QEs in this paradigm:

1. **Strategic Architects of Quality**
   QEs are increasingly seen as architects of quality, designing and implementing robust quality processes that are integral to the development lifecycle from the outset. They set quality standards and guidelines that align with Shift Left principles, ensuring that quality measures are baked into the product development from the beginning.
2. **Collaboration and Communication Catalysts**
   QEs facilitate vital communication and collaboration across various teams, including development, operations, and testing. Their role as intermediaries helps to ensure that all stakeholders are aligned on quality objectives, making quality a collective responsibility across all phases of project development.
3. **Proactive Involvement in Planning**
   Early involvement in project planning allows QEs to inject quality-focused strategies at every phase. They provide crucial insights into potential quality risks and appropriate testing strategies, significantly shaping the development process to preemptively tackle potential issues.
4. **Educators on Effective Testing Techniques**
   QEs are responsible for guiding the team on effective testing techniques, such as during unit testing and integration testing. Their

expertise helps other team members understand and implement practices that contribute to early defect detection, enhancing the overall software quality.

5. **Test Automation Strategists**

   QEs play a pivotal role in devising and refining the test automation strategy. While developers should be the main contributors in the actual development and maintenance of test scripts, QEs identify key opportunities for automation, guide the selection of appropriate tools and methods, and oversee the integration of automated testing into the continuous integration and delivery pipeline. This strategic oversight aligns test automation with broader project goals and efficiently enhances the development cycle.

6. **Champions of Continuous Learning and Improvement**

   Staying updated with the latest in testing technologies, tools, and methodologies is essential for QEs. They leverage this knowledge to drive continual improvement in testing practices, adopting innovative solutions that enhance both efficiency and effectiveness.

7. **Performance and Scalability Testing Experts**

   In collaboration with other team members, QEs plan and execute performance and scalability tests. This involves assessing how the application behaves under various load conditions and verifying that it meets the set performance benchmarks, which is crucial for user satisfaction and system reliability.

8. **Facilitators of Shift Left Training and Onboarding**
QEs develop comprehensive training programs and onboarding processes to instill a shift-left mindset across the team. They help all team members grasp the importance of early testing and equip them to uphold quality standards throughout the development process.

As the digital landscape continues to evolve, the role of QEs will expand beyond traditional boundaries. They will become central figures in strategic planning, risk management, and advocacy for best practices in quality engineering. Their ability to adapt and lead in this dynamic environment will be crucial for organizations aiming to maintain high standards of software quality and reliability.

In this way, QEs not only contribute to the technical aspects of quality assurance but also drive cultural shifts within organizations, emphasizing quality as a collective responsibility that begins at the earliest stages of project conception. This holistic approach not only improves product quality but also enhances team cohesion and project outcomes.

Emerging Responsibilities of QEs

As Quality Engineering (QE) continues to evolve, Quality Engineers are stepping into more strategic and transformational roles that are crucial for the future of software quality assurance:

- **Integration of CI/CD, Testing Infrastructure, and Cloud Solutions.** Quality Engineers are spearheading the integration and optimization of Continuous Integration and Continuous Delivery/Deployment (CI/CD) methodologies, testing infrastructures, and cloud-based environments. These technological advancements support agile development practices and enable seamless continuous integration, delivery, and deployment, leading to faster time-to-market and more reliable software release cycles.
- **Strategic Planning.** Quality Engineers are utilizing AI-driven analytics to enhance efficiency and effectiveness within testing and quality assurance operations. They are tasked with developing detailed quality roadmaps that align testing strategies with overarching business goals and the latest technological innovations, including artificial intelligence. These roadmaps are essential for guiding teams towards adopting more effective and efficient testing practices.

- **Risk Management.** In their expanded role, Quality Engineers focus on the early detection and mitigation of potential risks associated with functionality, performance, and security. Employing advanced testing techniques and leveraging AI-driven predictive analytics, they are able to anticipate issues before they manifest, allowing for more strategic allocation of testing resources and better overall software quality.
- **Observability and Monitoring.** Quality Engineers are configuring and maintaining sophisticated AI-driven monitoring and logging systems to deliver real-time insights into application performance and user experience. They promote the use of these systems and establish robust feedback loops to facilitate continuous improvement based on AI-analyzed monitoring data and user feedback.
- **AI-driven Automation.** Overseeing the implementation of AI technologies, Quality Engineers manage the development and integration of automated testing tools that enhance test case generation and script automation. This shift not only streamlines the testing process but also significantly boosts testing accuracy and efficiency.
- **User-oriented Testing.** Quality Engineers advocate for the importance of usability and accessibility testing conducted by real users.

This approach ensures that software products not only meet technical specifications but also align with user expectations and accessibility standards, providing a more inclusive user experience.

By embracing these technological and methodological advancements, Quality Engineers are not only enhancing their own strategic capabilities but also driving broader innovations and efficiencies in software development practices across various industries. Their pivotal role in shaping the future landscape of Quality Engineering underscores the importance of their contributions to achieving high-quality software products that meet both current and future demands. This ongoing transformation positions Quality Engineers at the forefront of industry advancements, ready to tackle emerging challenges with expertise and foresight.

TRANSFORMING QUALITY MANAGERS

As the future of software development continues to evolve rapidly, the role of Quality Managers is undergoing a profound transformation. These professionals are no longer confined to traditional managerial duties; they are increasingly becoming dynamic catalysts for change within their organizations. Recognizing the critical importance of quality in product development, companies are investing more than ever in nurturing or recruiting Quality Managers who are not just leaders, but also hands-on technical contributors.

In the future, this trend is expected to intensify, particularly in companies that embrace remote work arrangements. The ability to effectively manage distributed teams and navigate technical challenges remotely will become paramount. While soft skills such as communication and leadership will remain essential, there will be a growing emphasis on technical proficiency among Quality Managers.

The integration of Artificial Intelligence (AI) technologies is set to redefine the capabilities of Quality Managers further. AI's application in predictive analytics and machine learning can enhance decision-making processes by providing insights derived from data patterns that might not be visible to the human eye. Quality Managers will not only leverage AI tools to predict potential quality issues before they become apparent, enabling proactive management of software quality, but they will also need to understand how these tools work internally. This deeper understanding will allow them to tune AI tools specifically for their projects and guide their teams more effectively through the nuances of AI implementation.

AI will also automate routine and complex tasks, allowing Quality Managers to focus on strategic initiatives such as improving process efficiencies and innovation. This shift will require them to gain a robust understanding of AI technologies and their implications on quality assurance practices. As AI continues to advance, Quality Managers must keep pace with these technologies to effectively lead their teams and drive quality across the development lifecycle.

Moreover, the evolving nature of managerial roles will extend beyond Quality Managers to encompass higher positions such as Directors of Engineering. Job descriptions for these senior leadership roles will increasingly include requirements for hands-on involvement in technical tasks. This shift reflects a recognition that leaders at all levels must possess a deep understanding of the technical intricacies of their domain to effectively guide their teams toward success.

In essence, the role of Quality Managers in the future will transcend traditional managerial boundaries. They will not only be leaders but also active contributors to the technical excellence of their teams. By blending their managerial skills with technical expertise, particularly in AI, they will empower their organizations to thrive in the dynamic landscape of modern software development.

This transformation signifies a future where Quality Managers are pivotal in driving innovation, upholding high standards of quality, and maintaining the agility needed to adapt to ever-changing technological advancements. AI technologies will be at the heart of this transformation, providing the tools necessary for Quality Managers to excel in their evolving roles.

ETHICAL CONSIDERATIONS IN AI AND QUALITY ENGINEERING

As Artificial Intelligence (AI) becomes increasingly integral to Quality Engineering (QE), the roles of Quality Engineers are evolving dramatically. These changes introduce not only advanced capabilities but also complex ethical considerations that are essential for maintaining integrity and effectiveness in QE practices. Here are the key ethical challenges and responsibilities that Quality Engineers must address:

1. Addressing Bias and Ensuring Fairness

Algorithmic Impartiality. AI systems may unintentionally reinforce existing biases if not meticulously designed. Quality Engineers are tasked with ensuring that AI models are trained using datasets that are both diverse and representative. This approach helps to minimize biases and aims to achieve equitable outcomes throughout all testing processes.

Equitable Testing Protocols. It is essential for Quality Engineers to develop testing procedures that are fair and non-discriminatory, ensuring that all demographic groups are represented appropriately and that no irrelevant user characteristics influence the results.

2. Safeguarding Data Privacy and Security

Secure Data Handling. Given that AI often processes large volumes of sensitive information, it's imperative that this data is managed securely and ethically. Robust measures must be in place to prevent data breaches and unauthorized access.

Compliance with Regulations. Quality Engineers must ensure that AI-driven processes adhere to relevant data privacy laws and industry standards, protecting user privacy and maintaining regulatory compliance.

3. Promoting Transparency and Accountability

Understandable AI Decisions. AI should not operate as a black box. Quality Engineers must ensure that the decision-making processes of AI systems are transparent and comprehensible to all stakeholders, fostering trust and clarity. Quality Engineers (QEs) may not build AI models, but they play a crucial role in promoting the use of explainability techniques to ensure AI decisions are transparent. Here's how they can address this:

1. **Advocacy.** QEs can advocate for the implementation of explainability methods like LIME (Local Interpretable Model-agnostic Explanations) or SHAP (SHapley Additive exPlanations) in AI projects.
2. **Collaboration.** They can work closely with data scientists and developers to ensure models include transparent decision-making processes.
3. **Quality Assurance.** QEs can ensure that AI systems are documented thoroughly and that their decision-making processes are clearly communicated to stakeholders.

By promoting these practices, QEs can help make AI systems more understandable and trustworthy.

Clear Accountability Structures. When AI decisions significantly impact users, there must be clear lines of accountability. Quality Engineers need to ensure that there are mechanisms for human oversight and intervention when necessary.

Developing Ethical Frameworks and Guidelines

Creating Ethical Guidelines. Organizations should establish specific ethical guidelines for the use of AI in QE. These guidelines should address potential biases, promote transparency, and define accountability measures.

Conducting Ethical Audits. Regular ethical audits and assessments are crucial to verify compliance with these guidelines. Practices should be adapted as needed to address emerging ethical challenges.

Inclusive Decision-Making. Decision-making processes should incorporate diverse perspectives by involving a wide range of stakeholders, especially when addressing ethical considerations in AI use within QE. An ethics committee or board can provide expertise and guidance on complex ethical issues, ensuring that ethical practices are maintained and reviewed regularly.

Continuous Education and Training. Quality Engineers should receive ongoing training on ethical AI use, equipping them to handle ethical dilemmas and implement best practices effectively.

Staying Informed on AI Ethics. Keeping up-to-date with the latest developments in AI ethics is crucial. Quality Engineers must continuously refine and improve their practices to adhere to the highest ethical standards.

By addressing these ethical challenges and responsibilities, Quality Engineers can help to ensure that AI integration into QE is done in a manner that is fair, transparent, secure, and beneficial to all stakeholders.

Balancing Innovation with Ethical Considerations

The future of QE is bound to the continuous integration of AI and emerging technologies, making it essential for Quality Engineers to maintain a balance between innovation and ethical responsibility. This balance is crucial not only for fostering technological advancements but also for upholding the dignity and rights of all users affected by these technologies.

By focusing on ethical AI development and fostering an organizational culture that prioritizes ethical considerations alongside technological advancements, Quality Engineers can lead their teams toward a future where both product quality and ethical integrity are held in the highest regard.

PERSONAL STORY: HOW AI REVOLUTIONIZED MY ROLE AS HEAD OF QUALITY ENGINEERING

As the Head of Quality Engineering, my work-days were once packed with challenges—attending back-to-back meetings, managing extensive follow-ups, reviewing dozens of reports, and maintaining top-notch software testing standards. However, the integration of Artificial Intelligence (AI) into our processes has dramatically transformed my daily routine, significantly boosting both efficiency and effectiveness.

Early Mornings with AI Insights

Now, my day begins with AI-generated reports that analyze the previous day's testing activities. Displayed directly on our dashboards for all team members to see, these reports highlight key findings and potential root causes. This approach not only saves significant time but also enables us to promptly pinpoint and address critical issues right from the start of the day.

Streamlined Communications

A significant change is the reduction in daily meetings, which were previously filled with extensive note-taking and action item follow-ups. AI tools equipped with voice recognition capabilities now capture meeting details, automatically generate summaries, and identify action items. This allows our meetings to commence with discussions on areas highlighted by AI, enabling us to focus more on strategic deliberations rather than routine documentation.

Personal Development and Mentorship

AI has also reshaped how I approach personal development within my team. With routine tasks now automated, I dedicate more time to enhancing my team's skills and fostering a culture of innovation. This shift has not only boosted our performance but also heightened job satisfaction and engagement.

Improved Work-Life Balance

Moreover, AI has significantly improved my work-life balance. By automating repetitive tasks, I manage my responsibilities more efficiently, which has cut down on overtime and reduced stress. This change has afforded me more quality time with family and for personal pursuits, leading to a healthier and more satisfying life overall.

Conclusion

The impact of AI on my role as a Quality Engineering Manager has been profoundly positive. It has not only streamlined our operations but also deepened my engagement with my team and personal life. Adopting AI was a transformative decision that has reshaped my professional landscape, making every day more productive and rewarding.

CONCLUSION

From my early fascination with software development and quality to navigating the transformative evolution of Quality Engineering (QE) amidst technological advancements, modern methodologies, and the rise of AI, my journey has been shaped by passion and innovation. Sitting in front of a Pravetz-8C, a Bulgarian Apple II clone, almost 30 years ago, I wrote and troubleshooted my first program in BASIC to display a snowflake, sparking my lifelong dedication to excellence in software. This book has explored the dynamics of navigating quality engineering in the AI era, offering insights into foundational principles, contemporary techniques, emerging challenges, and future trends. I continue to inspire and lead, pushing boundaries to shape the future of software development with an unwavering commitment to quality and innovation.

Reflecting on the Journey

Foundations of Quality Engineering. Understanding the roots of QE, from its inception to its current state, is crucial. The shift from traditional quality management to the dynamic, collaborative, and early-integration-focused "Shift Left" paradigm has set the stage for modern quality practices. These foundational principles have paved the way for a more integrated and proactive approach to quality, emphasizing early testing, continuous collaboration, and risk mitigation.

Techniques and Strategies in Quality Engineering. The integration of Agile and DevOps has revolutionized QE, fostering a culture of collaboration, speed, and continuous improvement. Automated testing, powered by AI, has enhanced efficiency and accuracy, enabling QE teams to focus on more strategic tasks. The embrace of continuous testing and the integration of testing into CI/CD pipelines have underscored the importance of real-time feedback and iterative improvement.

Challenges and Solutions in Quality Engineering. Navigating the complexities of change management and addressing the talent crunch in hiring quality engineers are pivotal challenges. By fostering a culture of continuous learning and development, organizations can adapt to these changes and build resilient QE teams. The role of Quality Engineers has evolved to encompass not just testing but also strategic planning, risk management, and advocacy for quality practices.

Future Trends and Innovations. AI stands at the forefront of future QE innovations, offering capabilities in predictive analytics, automated testing, and intelligent defect management. However, the integration of AI brings forth ethical considerations that must be addressed to uphold fairness, transparency, and accountability. As we look to the future, balancing innovation with ethical responsibility will be paramount.

Final Thoughts

The journey of Quality Engineering (QE) is one of continuous evolution and adaptation. As we move forward, the convergence of AI, DevOps, and proactive quality assurance practices will shape the future of software development. Quality Engineers will continue to play a critical role, not just as testers but as enablers of quality throughout the software development lifecycle.

It's understandable that the rapid integration of AI might evoke apprehension among Quality Engineers, who may fear that their roles could become redundant. However, it's important to remember that our industry has always been evolving. Much like the introduction of test automation, AI will not eliminate the need for Quality Engineers but will instead enhance their capabilities, enabling them to become even more effective champions of quality within their organizations.

By embracing new technologies, fostering collaboration, and maintaining a commitment to ethical practices, QE professionals can drive continuous improvement and deliver high-quality software that meets the evolving needs of users and businesses. The future of QE is not just about survival. It's about flourishing, with numerous opportunities to innovate, enhance, and excel.

This book has offered a roadmap for understanding and adapting to these profound changes. It has emphasized the importance of a holistic approach that integrates technology, methodology, and ethics. As we navigate this dynamic landscape, the principles and strategies outlined will serve as a guide for Quality Engineers, helping them to thrive and succeed in the era of AI-driven quality engineering.

ABOUT THE AUTHOR

Evgeny Tkachenko is a seasoned expert in quality engineering, with nearly two decades of leadership in quality management, test automation, and release management. His professional journey has spanned significant tenures at globally renowned companies such as EPAM Systems, Wayfair, and Amazon. Throughout his career, Evgeny has spearheaded initiatives across diverse sectors including telecommunications, financial services, healthcare, and online entertainment, consistently delivering high-quality products. His dedication and expertise have established him as a pivotal figure in shaping the future of Quality Engineering.

Widely recognized within the Quality Engineering community, Evgeny is a regular speaker at prestigious international conferences, where he shares insights that resonate with and motivate industry professionals. He also contributes his expertise to various international publications, enriching the field with his profound knowledge on software testing and quality.

Beyond his technical and managerial skills, Evgeny is an esteemed author and a visionary thought leader, deeply committed to advancing the discipline of quality engineering. His work does not just encompass the practical aspects of quality assurance but also extends to shaping the strategic future of the field. Through his influential writings and speeches, Evgeny champions the cause of excellence in software quality assurance, continually pushing the boundaries to innovate and improve within the industry.

Evgeny values the feedback and insights from his readers. If you wish to provide feedback on this book or discuss its contents, please feel free to connect with him through his LinkedIn profile:

https://www.linkedin.com/in/evgenytka4enko/

ACKNOWLEDGEMENTS

I am deeply grateful to the incredible teams I have had the privilege to lead over the past two decades at Innova Distribution, EPAM Systems, Wayfair, One Medical, and Amazon. Your dedication, resilience, and willingness to embrace challenging yet interesting transformations have been a source of inspiration for me. Thank you for allowing me to navigate these journeys with you and for your unwavering commitment to excellence.

To my family, thank you for your endless support and belief in me. Your encouragement and understanding have been the bedrock of my professional and personal growth. I couldn't have achieved any of this without your love and patience.

I would also like to extend my heartfelt thanks to Dorothy Graham, James Whittaker, Michael Bolton, James Bach, and Lisa Crispin. Your books, presentations, and publications have been a wellspring of inspiration and knowledge. Your contributions to the field of software testing and quality assurance have profoundly shaped my thinking and approach.

A special thank you to Dorothy Graham once again, for not only reviewing this book but also for your ongoing support and guidance throughout the years. Your insights and mentorship have been invaluable, and I am incredibly grateful for your contributions to this work and to my professional journey.

Finally, to all my colleagues, friends, and mentors who have supported me along the way, thank you. Your encouragement and wisdom have been instrumental in my journey, and I am deeply appreciative of the impact you have had on my life and career.

SOURCES

Books:

- Bridges, W. (1991). *Managing Transitions: Making the Most of Change.* Da Capo Lifelong Books.
- Crosby, P. B. (1979). *Quality is Free.* McGraw-Hill.
- Crispin, L., & Gregory, J. (2009). *Agile Testing: A Practical Guide for Testers and Agile Teams.* Addison-Wesley Professional.
- Cohn, M. (2010). Succeeding with Agile: Software Development Using Scrum. Addison-Wesley Professional.
- Kotter, J. P. (1996). *Leading Change.* Boston: Harvard Business School Press.
- Forsgren, N., Humble, J., & Kim, G. (2018). *Accelerate: The Science of Lean Software and DevOps: Building and Scaling High Performing Technology Organizations.* Portland, OR: IT Revolution Press.
- Coeckelbergh, M. (2020). *AI Ethics.* The MIT Press.
- Marr, B. (2019). *Artificial Intelligence in Practice: How 50 Successful Companies Used AI and Machine Learning to Solve Problems.* Wiley.
- Deming, W. Edwards. *Out of the Crisis.* MIT Press, 1986.

- Whittaker, J. (2009). *Exploratory Software Testing: Tips, Tricks, Tours, and Techniques to Guide Test Design.* Addison-Wesley.
- Scott, Cynthia D., and Dennis T. Jaffe. *Managing Change at Work: Leading People Through Organizational Transitions.* Crisp Publications, 1995

Articles:

- Müller, V. C. (2020). Ethics of Artificial Intelligence and Robotics. In E. N. Zalta (Ed.), *The Stanford Encyclopedia of Philosophy* (Spring 2020 Edition). Metaphysics Research Lab, Stanford University. https://plato.stanford.edu/entries/ethics-ai/
- Beer, M., & Nohria, N. (2000). *Cracking the code of change.* Harvard Business Review. https://hbr.org/2000/05/cracking-the-code-of-change
- Gartner. (2023). *Changing Change Management.* https://emt.gartnerweb.com/ngw/globalassets/en/human-resources/documents/trends/changing-change-management.pdf
- CEB Corporate Leadership Council. (2021). *Open Source Change: Full Study.* https://pwchangetoolkit.wordpress.com/wp-content/uploads/2021/05/ceb_open_source_change_full_study-2-1.pdf
- WTW. (2023). *The Business Case for Change Management When Driving Organization*

- *Transformation.* https://www.wtwco.com/en-ph/insights/2023/05/the-business-case-for-change-management-when-driving-organization-transformation
- SmartBear. (n.d.). Automated Testing. SmartBear. https://smartbear.com/learn/automated-testing/
- Drive Research. (2023). New Year's resolutions statistics and trends. https://www.driveresearch.com/market-research-company-blog/new-years-resolutions-statistics/

Blog Posts:

- Gamba, S., & Graham, D. (n.d.). Test Automation Patterns Wiki. https://TestAutomationPatterns.org
- Dodds, K. (n.d.). The Testing Trophy and Testing Classifications. https://kentcdodds.com/blog/the-testing-trophy-and-testing-classifications
- Schaffer, A. (2018). Testing of Microservices. https://engineering.atspotify.com/2018/01/testing-of-microservices/
- Morville, P. (n.d.). User Experience Design. https://semanticstudios.com/user_experience_design/

- Scott, A. Testing Pyramids & Ice-Cream Cones. https://alisterscott.github.io/TestingPyramids.html
- Bolton, M. (2017, November). *The End of "Manual Testing"*. Retrieved from https://developsense.com/blog/2017/11/the-end-of-manual-testing.